VACCINE HESITANT

SURVIVING THE COVID-19 PANDEMIC

DR. VANCE G. MAKIN BSC (HONS),
MS, MD, FRCP(C)

VMIL PRESS

ISBN 978-1-7778721-1-3

Suggestions and comments may be sent to vmakinmd@gmail.com.

Front cover image courtesy of Alexey Solodovnikov (Idea, Producer, CG, Editor), Valeria Arkhipova (Scientific Consultant) (https://commons.wikimedia.org/wiki/File:Coronavirus._SARS-CoV-2.png), https: // creativecommons. org / licenses / by-sa / 4.0 / legalcode.

Rear cover image courtesy of National Institute of Allergy and Infectious Diseases.

Created with Vellum

For Suzanne and Jane

CONTENTS

ACKNOWLEDGMENTS

The author is indebted to Jane Makin and Valerie Makin-Rakoczy for proofreading, and to author Kirk Makin for general advice and sports analogy encouragement.

THE AUTHOR

Dr. V. Makin has several decades of experience as a clinical neurologist that includes explaining research trials, medical catastrophes and various other complex situations to patients, family members and students. He has degrees in biochemistry, molecular biology and medicine, and specialist certification in neurology. He has no political affiliation.

DISCLAIMER

The author and publisher are providing this book and its contents on an "as is" basis and make no representations or warranties of any kind with respect to this book or its contents. The author and publisher disclaim all such representations and warranties, including for example warranties of merchantability and healthcare for a particular purpose. In addition, the author and publisher do not represent or warrant that the information accessible via this book is accurate, complete or current.

Some statements made about products and services have not been evaluated by the US Food and Drug Administration or Health Canada. They are not intended to diagnose, treat, cure, or prevent any condition or disease. Please consult with your own physician or healthcare specialist regarding the suggestions and recommendations made in this book.

Except as specifically stated in this book, neither the author or publisher, nor any authors, contributors, or other representatives will be liable for damages arising out of or in connection with the use of this book. This is a comprehensive limitation of liability that applies to all damages of any kind, including (without limitation) compensatory;

CHAPTER 1

INTRODUCTION

ANOTHER DAMN'D THICK, SQUARE BOOK!

ALWAYS, SCRIBBLE, SCRIBBLE, SCRIBBLE! EH! MR. GIBBON?

KING GEORGE III

A near-biblical plague is devastating the world, including the United States, Indonesia, Brazil and even Antarctica.

In the US and Canada, up to 25% of people are legitimately vaccine-hesitant. They are intelligent and well-intentioned people who just want to base a decision on clear facts. Opinionated media personalities, self-serving statistics, and selective reporting are not helping.

This book is for them and anyone else who just wants to understand more about Covid-19.

Understanding the enemy is important. The initial chapters describe a Covid-19 infection as if it were a military operation, with specific tactics and strategies. Opportunities to us to resist Covid-19 at each stage are discussed. Readers in a hurry can skip directly to Chapter 6.

Other chapters review the benefits and risks of the North American vaccines. In each case, the odds of a good result are calculated as an objective benefit-to-risk ratio.

The book is rounded out by discussion of public health issues, distancing, breath filters (including "masks"), future variants, herd immunity, how Covid-19 differs from influenza and other recent epidemics, microchips, evaluating non-expert opinions, how governments and the World Health Organization were caught napping, whether our health care systems have been or will be overwhelmed, pregnancy, bioweapons, and other topics of interest.

~

Nietzsche said, “Good writers have two things in common: they prefer to be understood rather than admired; and they do not write for knowing and over-acute readers.” Everything in this book is easily open to verification. Many facts in this book could be quibbled over by the “over-acute” but this book is not intended for them.

CHAPTER 2

COVID-19'S BATTLE TACTICS

> The trouble with the world is that the stupid are cocksure and the intelligent are full of doubt.
>
> Bertrand Russell

Viruses are deadly serious about their business. They do not consciously think or plan but pretending that they do makes them easier to understand. They have only one purpose, which is to spread, and they take no prisoners.

Here is how a successful invasion and colonization of just one of your body's cells would occur, as ten separate tactics. Understanding them suggests possible avenues for resistance.

Summary

The molecular biology of Covid-19 attacks is complicated but well-understood. Understanding these stages presents various opportunities to resist it, some of which are surprisingly low-tech.

Tactic 1: On patrol

The Covid-19 virus, when outside of a human, has severe time constraints. Falling to the ground or having its protective bubble evaporate generally means it dies. As long as it can ride through the air in this bubble vehicle, it is armed and ready. These bubbles come in two sizes.

Droplets

Those called "droplets" are larger and are the heavy infantry. They travel only a few feet before settling by gravity and digging in wherever they land. While in the air, they can be inhaled into the nose, throat or bronchial tubes. Once they settle on a surface they can get onto your hands and from there your eyes, nose or mouth.

A sneeze releases droplets (seen falling towards the ground) and aerosol particles (seen suspended in the air).

Aerosols

Aerosol particles are the light infantry - smaller, able to range further and always ready for a quick skirmish. They move in air currents and can even be jostled by a passing nitrogen or oxygen molecule. They tend to evaporate quickly but are armed and very dangerous until then. Some extend their patrol life further by coalescing with other aerosol particles.

Aerosols are launched by a cough, sneeze, scream, loud speech or even quiet speech. Normal people are constantly emitting aerosols. If our vision permitted, we would see an aerosol cloud around everyone's head most of the time.

The virus's patrol radius increases if its droplet or aerosol vehicle is ejected at high velocity, such as with a cough or sneeze, or if it starts high off the ground, or if the air is humid. For a firsthand impression of how far an aerosol can range, ask someone to stand six feet away from you and squirt an aerosol air freshener upwards.

Success for a Covid-19 virus is when its droplet or aerosol particle is sucked into the humid and sheltered safe harbor of your nose.

Tactic 2: Set up a beachhead

Most patrols are futile and the virus dies. However, inefficiency is not a problem when you have billions of soldiers to squander. Eventually some are bound to find their way into an unsuspecting enemy nasopharynx (nose).

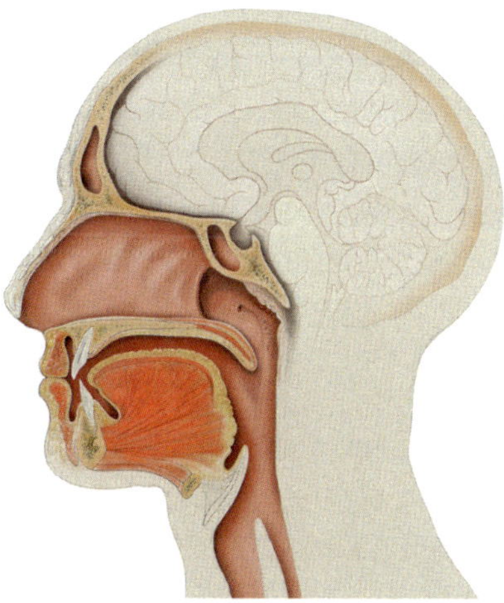

The nose, or nasopharynx, is more than just the facial feature called "the nose." It is a large air-filled space inside the head where air circulates and humidifies. In the image it is the large pink area in the centre. The nose provides a large surface area for invading Covid-19 viruses to land on once they enter through the nostrils.

In a typical setting, each infected person will eventually establish about 3 nasal beachheads in other people.[1] Using the figure of 3, this means that a single infected nose will enable the virus to invade, on average, three more noses. By the time the original virus has been wrestled to the ground by your immune system (discussed below), there will be three new virus invasions just starting out. Each of them will infect three more noses for a total of nine. This will be followed by 27, which will infect 9 more, then 81, 243, 729, etc. The Delta variant can spread even faster.

The safest harbor for Covid-19 is your nose. As soon as a droplet or aerosol particle contacts the moist surface of cells lining your nose, its worries about evaporation are over. This moistness evolved naturally to humidify our inhaled air and dissolve scent molecules and the Covid-19 virus learned to use it against us.

Tactic 3: Break in

Viruses cannot thrive very long in your nose, no matter how warm and cozy it may be. They are not self-sufficient, carry very little of their own equipment, and must invade a human cell as soon as possible. They start with the closest cells, which are the ones lining your nose. These moist, vulnerable cells are also easier to penetrate than, for example, the fortified exterior of a skin or bone cell.

The virus has two entry options - either break in by brute force or be clever and exploit an existing weakness. Virtually all successful Covid-19 invasions use the second option, exploiting an existing weakness. Specifically, they use a doorway that originally evolved for very different purposes, called the "ACE2 receptor."

Normal human cells are studded with many different protein molecules that serve various functions such as admitting specific chemicals or hormones into the interior of the cell. One of these doorways is the ACE2 receptor. Covid-19, and specifically its “spike protein”, has learned how to trick the ACE2 receptor and gain entry into the cell.

. . .

The ACE2 receptor and spike protein - catcher's mitt and tennis ball

The ACE2 receptor lives on the surface of human cells, patiently waiting for messages from other cells. It helps to think of the ACE2 receptor as a baseball catcher's mitt. The molecule it normally interacts with can be thought of as a baseball. As it turns out, a tennis ball can also fit, but there were no tennis balls around when it evolved so this was never relevant. Until 2019, that is. Then, in the course of one ordinary day in the life of an ordinary coronavirus inhabiting an ordinary animal, everything changed.

Coronaviruses are a class of virus named for their "corona" of spike proteins, as seen by electron microscopy. They inhabit various animals, including humans. This particular coronavirus's parents were studded with the usual spike proteins like a clove and orange pomander. Its spike proteins (cloves) had no affinity for the ACE2 receptor (catcher's mitt) of human cells, so it could not infect human cells.

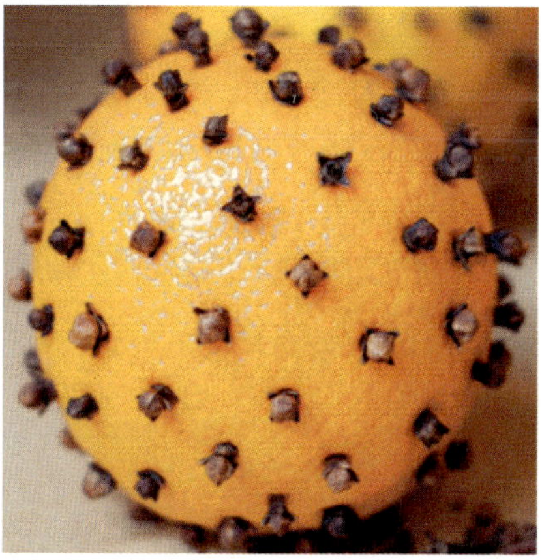

An orange and clove pomander looks like a Covid-19 virus with spike proteins.

Then one day, one of the animal coronavirus's spike proteins turned into something different in a process called "mutation". The new spike protein looked like a tennis ball.

Random mutations like this occur all the time with viruses. It is one consequence of having a million babies at a time. Most mutations are fatal. In all likelihood, mutations that made the spike proteins look like tennis balls had occurred many times before but they were dead ends. But one day, in Wuhan, China, this lucky mutant virus happened to enter the nose of a human.

Other animal coronaviruses had tried to set up a warm swampy beach-head in human noses millions of times and failed, but this time it was different. The mutant virus, now studded with tennis ball spike proteins instead of the old ones, met up with one of the human cells, whose ACE2 receptor catcher's mitt innocently reached out and caught it.

This hapless cell had never needed to know the difference between baseballs (its normal targets) and tennis balls (the new mutation), because tennis balls had not been invented yet. Now it was too late.

In no time, the ACE2 receptor's catcher's mitt transported the mutant coronavirus virus into the deep interior of the human cell. The mutant coronavirus probably would not have penetrated the cell without this help, but with a front door and a willing usher, it was simple.

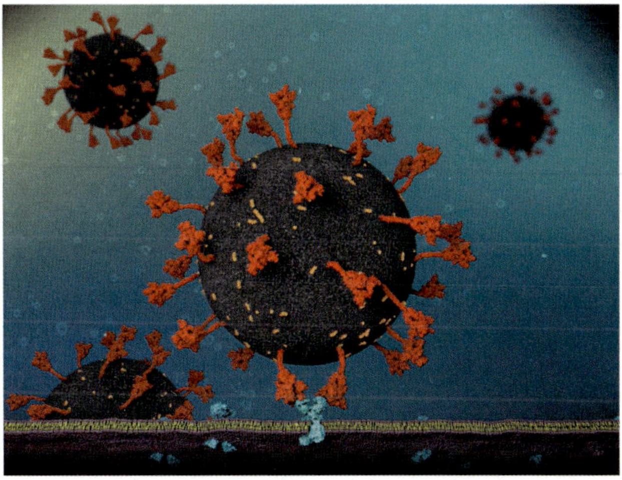

A human cell's ACE2 receptor (catcher's mitt, blue) snags a passing Covid-19 spike protein (tennis ball, red).

Once inside, the mutant coronavirus took over the cell and had the usual few million offspring (no sex required), all of whom had the same tennis ball spike protein mutation and therefore the same advantage.

The family changed its name to Covid-19 and started a dynasty.

Natural selection

This process of a new mutant having an advantage that allows it to spread to a new organism is billions of years old. Occasional new mutations will be able to have more offspring, spread faster, and eventually outbreed the older generation. This process is called natural selection, the mechanism underlying evolution. It is why grasshoppers are green - any pink or blue grasshoppers were eaten by birds before they could breed more of the same.

Covid-19 evolved this way and it continues to evolve. The Delta variant, for example, is another random mutation with a "selective advantage" over the original Covid-19 virus strain. It is now well on its way to replacing it.

A Covid-19 virus is about one ten-thousandth of a millimeter across. A nose cell is about one hundredth of a millimeter across. They both sound small but this is actually a huge size difference. For a Covid-19 virus that has found its way into a human nose cell, keeping the battle plans organized in this vast and busy place is essential.

Tactic 4: Review the battle plans

Covid-19 genome

The Covid-19 genome is the library of all the instructions needed to make a Covid-19 virus. It is kept in the form of a nucleic acid molecule called ribonucleic acid, or RNA. This genomic RNA (hereafter called gRNA) is not the same as messenger RNA (mRNA), which will be discussed below.[2]

A virus is little more than its minimalistic genome protected by some type of membrane or shell, with a few essential proteins in its backpack. It fully intends to steal everything else it needs from your human cell, and it cannot spawn new viruses any other way.

Human genome

The human genome is similar to the Covid-19 virus's although much larger and made of a slightly different nucleic acid called deoxyribonucleic acid, or DNA. Human cells are not all the same. Each cell contains the complete human genome but it is only expressed in specific ways in each of our 250 different types of cell. One of these cell types is the wet swampy cells lining the nose. They express genes for producing mucus rather than ones producing bone, for example.

. . .

Cells

A cell is the basic building block of human bodies. Each one has a genome and a protective covering. Animal cells also have what a virus can only covet, their own machinery for tasks such as energy production and making proteins.

Proteins

Proteins are large molecules whose three dimensional shape determines their function. Our normal genome carries the codes for tens of thousands of different proteins. Each has a unique shape and function. Some interact with other proteins or smaller chemicals whose shapes are compatible, like the ACE2 receptor (catcher's mitt). Others are consumable building blocks, like bricks and mortar, that go to building structures. Proteins that catalyze biochemical reactions are also very important.[3] Finally, there are those that act as midwives for assembling the next generation of cells or viruses.

Messenger RNA (mRNA)

In human cells, the genome does not talk directly to the ribosomal protein factory where proteins are actually made. It remains aloof and sends blueprints in the form of short RNA molecules. Because of this messaging function they are called "messenger" RNA, or mRNA. There is one messenger RNA for each protein.

Covid-19 needs to hijack this system so it slyly evolved a way to make its genomic RNA (gRNA) look like a normal human messenger RNA (mRNA) molecule. As soon as the Covid-19 virus genome enters the cell it goes straight to the protein factories, acts like an mRNA, and certain important proteins get immediately fabricated. Chief amongst these proteins is "replicase", to be discussed further below.

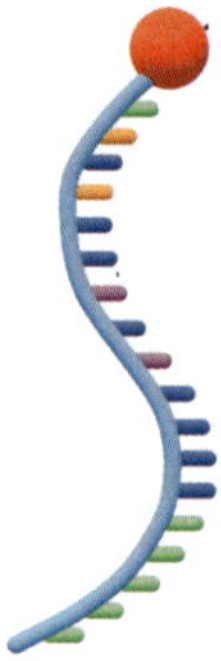

A messenger RNA molecule - the protein-making code is in the colored pegs.

Ribosome protein factories

A normal human cell's ribosomes will take instructions from any appropriately formatted mRNA and crank out the corresponding protein molecule. They naively assume any mRNA molecules that drop by must have come from the human genome.

An important question is whether we, too, can trick our ribosomal protein factories with laboratory-made mRNA molecules of our own design.[4]

Ribosomes (brown) move along the messenger RNA molecules from left to right, reading its code (colored pegs) and converting the code to a steadily growing new protein (colored balls).

In theory, each step in the protein building procedure is a potential target for a drug to interfere with it. However, as most of these processes are really those of the human cell itself, and only hijacked by the invading Covid-19 virus, shutting them down with a drug would also damage normal (uninfected) human cells. This makes it difficult to find safe drugs to stop Covid-19 once it is inside. Perimeter defense, killing the virus while it is still in nasal mucus and before it breaches the cell's inner sanctum, is easier.

As mentioned above, this willingness on the part of ribosomes to turn any properly formatted messenger RNA into a protein raises the possibility that we might be able to make mRNA molecules in the lab and sneak them into cells. This is the basis of a brand new technology to fight Covid-19, to be discussed below.

Tactic 5: Fabricate new Covid-19 genomes

This part is complicated but only because the Covid-19 virus is tricky. Although its genome is made of genomic RNA (gRNA), Covid-19 has disguised it to look like a normal human messenger RNA (mRNA) molecule, to fool the ribosomal protein factory. This may sound confusing but it is the end product of natural selection minimizing the trouble a virus has to go to when it invades a cell. The Covid-19 genome, now looking and acting like any old messenger RNA (mRNA) molecule rather than the deadly interloper it is, is quickly translated by ribosomes into a special Covid-19 protein that is essential for the next step, called replicase.

The Covid-19 genomic RNA (gRNA) code for these three proteins is written in correct direction for ribosomes to immediately use, called the "sense" order. [5]

However, to make more virus genomes, a mirror image "antisense" template needs to be made. The antisense version can then mass produce millions of new sense gRNA genomes, one for each future offspring Covid-19 virus. This process is similar to using a photographic negative to produce prints or a metal die to stamp out parts.

This procedure completely bypasses any use of DNA by the Covid-19 virus. All animal cells, and many viruses, use DNA to store their genetic archive. The advantage for Covid-19 of skipping a DNA backup is that it eliminates steps. The disadvantage is that there is no reference backup copy of the Covid-19 genetic code in case of mistakes.

Replicase

The enzyme required to make the antisense genomic gRNA template is called replicase, because it helps replicate the genome.[6] The human cell cannot supply replicase as it does not have the gene for it, having never required this process for itself. Covid-19 has to bring the gene along and makes it the first priority. Soon after entering a cell, Covid-19 has tricked the ribosomes and produced replicase protein.

Two other immediately manufactured proteins help keep the new RNA genomes organized and correct any errors, but are beyond the scope of this book.

The sense RNA genome (grey) enters Replicase's mouth. When it exits there is also an antisense version (purple).

Tactic 6: Commandeer supplies and energy

The Covid-19 viruses have no means of energy or chemical production and need to steal them from the infected cell. The necessary chemicals to make proteins and other compounds are also stolen.

Tactic 7: Fabricate other proteins

So far the Covid-19 genome (gRNA) has entered the cell via the ACE2 receptor doorway, then posed as an mRNA molecule to trick the ribosomal protein factory into making replicase. The replicase has produced many antisense genomic (gRNA) molecules, which have been used as templates to produce more sense genomes, one of which will end up inside each member of the next generation of Covid-19 viruses.

There is still the problem of making the other proteins that Covid-19 will need. These include the bricks and mortar to make the shells of new viruses and a few others. Only replicase was made directly from the genomic RNA (gRNA) pretending to be an mRNA, so how do these other proteins get made?

It turns out that the antisense genome copies have a second function. The first was to serve as templates for making new sense gRNA molecules, as described above. The other function is to act as messenger RNA (mRNA) molecules themselves that direct the ribosomal protein factory into making these other proteins. Amongst these are the E, M and N proteins (the function of which is beyond the scope of this book), and also the critically important spike protein, which is destined to fool a future uninfected cell's catcher's mitt ACE2 receptors into admitting it into a cell.

To summarize, the Covid-19 virus injects a sense gRNA molecule into the human cell. It poses as an mRNA and immediately directs construction of replicase by the ribosomes. The replicase then makes numerous antisense copies of the gRNA. These antisense genomes do two different things to produce the final products needed for new viruses. The first is to serve as templates to make more sense copies of gRNA. The second is to be processed into mRNA molecules that direct the synthesis of all the rest of the proteins needed to build new Covid-19 viruses.

Tactic 8: Muster

As the Covid-19 genomes and spike proteins accumulate inside the doomed human cell, they receive their armored exterior of "capsid" proteins. They are marshalled and assembled into active new virus particles, eager to go out hunting on their own.

A fully assembled Covid-19 virus showing the RNA genome (black line) and the spike proteins (green). The blue circles and pink triangles are other proteins beyond the scope of this book.

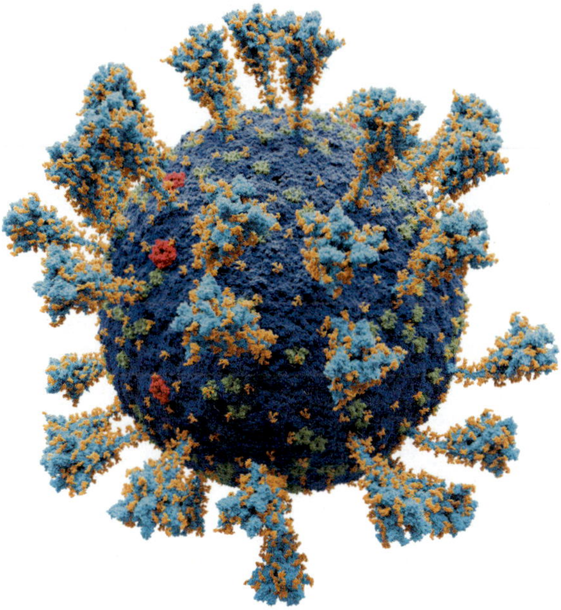

Exterior view of a new Covid-19 virus sporting its coat of armor "capsid" proteins (dark blue); and spike proteins (light blue and orange).

Tactic 9: Break out

Once enough new Covid-19 virus particles have been mustered the cell releases them and they flood the area. Some will find their way to other cells in the same victim's body, to take over and abuse the same way. Others, leaving on what is usually a suicide mission, are destined to patrol outside the original victim's body on an aerosol or droplet bubble, looking for new victims.

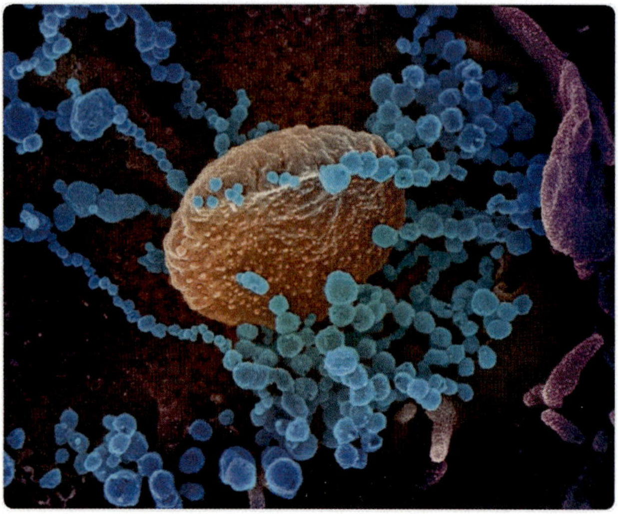

New Covid-19 viruses (blue) breaking out of a doomed cell (orange). Most will die. Some will go on to infect other cells in the same human. Some will exit the body, perhaps in a sneeze, and look for new victims.

Tactic 10: On patrol again

To find new victims, the legions of new Covid-19 viruses now waiting in the nasal mucus on the outside of the nose cells must travel. They do so mostly by air, with the hope of getting inhaled by a new unsuspecting human. To help with this task, a sneeze or a cough would be ideal but is not essential. Humans evolved the sneeze and cough reflexes to keep their airways clear, but the virus subverts them for its own selfish purpose of breaking out on aerosol and droplet rafts. Even normal speech will produce droplets and aerosols, accounting for why it is so infectious.

The Covid-19 viruses position themselves in the airway, especially the nose, and wait. There they sit, comfily surrounded by warm, fragrant mucus until they are suddenly launched in your direction by something as unobtrusive as normal speech. This starts the clock running on finding a new beachhead before their bubbles evaporate or fall to the floor. A fortunate few viruses will manage to find new victims and start the own families.

Molecular biology roundup

It is important to know your enemy. This chapter is the longest and most complex, but that is what makes molecular biology fun. Here is a roundup:

1. Covid-19 genomic RNA (gRNA) enters the human cell through the ACE2 receptor doorway.

2. It immediately poses as an mRNA in order to get replicase made.

3. Replicase turns the gRNA into an antisense copy.

4. The antisense copy does two things. First, it is a template for making more sense gRNA genomes. Second, it is processed into mRNA molecules that go off to make other proteins (like the E, M and N proteins) and the all-important spike protein.

5. There is a general accumulation of sense genomes and these proteins, which assemble themselves into new Covid-19 viruses.

6. The offspring viruses leave the cells and look for uninfected cells to invade.

---

1. The number 3 is called the R0. It was 1.5 in January 2020 and ranged as high as 7 since then. The average has been about 2-3. It is discussed further in Chapters 18 and 19.
2. Two other types of RNA, called transfer RNA and ribosomal RNA, are beyond the scope of this book.
3. All of our biochemistry is dependent on catalysts (enzymes). They facilitate reactions that could otherwise not occur at body temperature. After the reaction occurs, the enzyme moves on to facilitate another one.
4. We can - see Chapter 7.
5. The code is written with four letters, A,T, G and C. Each of them has a specific partner - A with T, and G with C. If a code was AGT, then the mirror image would be TCA. These are called the sense and antisense sequences, respectively.
6. Replicate means to make new copies of the original genome (gRNA). Replicase is also called RNA-dependent RNA polymerase or RdRp.

CHAPTER 3

HOW TO RESIST COVID-19'S TACTICS

> COLLECTIVE FEAR STIMULATES HERD INSTINCT, AND TENDS TO PRODUCE FEROCITY TOWARD THOSE WHO ARE NOT REGARDED AS MEMBERS OF THE HERD.
>
> BERTRAND RUSSELL

The reason for considering Covid-19's tactics one by one is to recognize opportunities to resist them. At the time of publication, there are no really effective drugs that cure Covid-19. The most effective measures come from understanding the physics of droplets and aerosols, and understanding the immune system.

Summary

Safe opportunities to resist Covid-19 invasion tactics occur mainly at the stage of inhaling it (use a filter), when it first establishes a beachhead (train the immune system to respond without delay) and when exhaling infectious particles (use a filter).

Resistance to Tactic 1 (on patrol)

Keep your distance

If Covid-19 virus-laden aerosols are in your vicinity you are a sitting duck. The best options are to leave the area or, at a minimum, stay upwind. It is usually impossible to know if an asymptomatic spreader is somewhere around you as he or she does not know, either. The prudent action would be to avoid getting close to any other people whose immune status is unknown.

This is an unfortunate change in lifestyle for everyone. Some people refuse to do it. They may feel they are being forced by others to maintain this distance but the fact is that we live in a different world now. It has become dangerous to be close to unknown people unless you, yourself, are immune. This will change someday, but we are not there yet.

Filter what you inhale

Filtering out aerosols just before they enter your nose or mouth is another possible intervention, using materials that stop the passage of droplets and aerosols. They work by a combination of tiny pore size and electrostatic attraction, similar to dust filters.

Resistance to Tactics 2 and 3 (set up a beachhead; break in)

Your personal nasal swamp, which might seem unimportant or even annoying to you, is a Covid-19 virus's dream vacation.

If a single Covid-19 virus has landed in your nose, now is the best time to destroy it, not after it has entered cells, replicated and created a new generation of viruses. Perimeter defense is always the best security. It will be conducted by your own automated nose sentries, the IgG antibodies of your immune system. Think of them as smart weapons.

. . .

Antibodies and pitcher's mitts

With IgG antibodies roaming around your nose looking for spike proteins (tennis balls), any Covid-19 viruses trying to establish a beachhead will be quickly mopped up. But the antibodies are not naturally there, they have to be trained. The first training session takes 14 days, during which you are infected and might not even survive.

These IgG antibodies are the pitcher's mitts discussed earlier. They are not quite the same as the catcher's mitts (the ACE2 receptors) but are close enough to catch the Covid-19 virus and its spike protein tennis balls.

Once the initial training has occurred, whenever these IgG antibody smart weapons spot a Covid-19 spike protein in the future they will recognize it as a call to action. A flood of new IgG antibodies will quickly enter the scene. It will no longer take 14 days because now they are already trained and just need to deploy.

The cell's normal ACE2 receptor (catcher's mitt) catches its normal target (baseball).

Unfortunately, the cell's normal ACE2 receptor (catcher's mitt) can also catch a Covid-19 spike protein (tennis ball).

After 14 days, IgG antibodies (pitcher's gloves) flood the scene to mop up all the tennis balls (spike proteins) on Covid-19 viruses.

The nightmare scenario is a new Covid-19 spike protein that looks like a football, caught by the ACE2 receptor (catcher's mitt) but not the IgG antibody pitcher's mitt. All previous immunity, natural or vaccine-induced, is lost.

The IgG antibodies catch these tennis balls and glue them together, cordon off their spike proteins, and help signal other parts of the immune system to join the battle. As long as Covid-19 invaders are in reasonably small numbers, they are quickly nuked by this perimeter defense and get no further.

There are actually three types of antibody. IgM antibodies are a general purpose first responder and are quickly available, but often not enough to do the job. IgA antibodies specialize in nose and airways sanitation but take a few days to intervene. The heavy artillery is the IgG antibodies, highly specific for the spike protein but unfortunately needing two weeks to be manufactured to order.

Is there room for improvement?

The IgG antibody system is incredibly effective but has one big flaw - the 14 days required for an initial response. You could become extremely ill or die during these two weeks, and you will likely pass it on to others. It turns out there is a way to bypass this delay, to the huge advantage of humans. It will be discussed in Chapter 7 and is currently our single best defense against this predator.

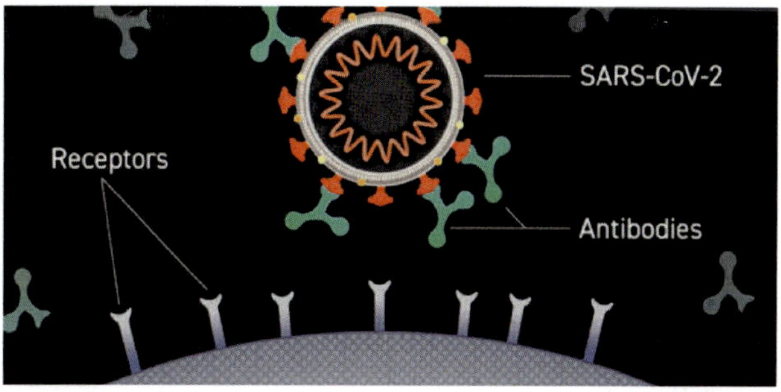

The lilac catcher's mitts (ACE2 receptors) reach out for the red tennis balls (Covid-19 spike proteins). They are foiled by the free-floating and ubiquitous green pitcher's mitts that are the IgG antibodies. Once antibodies stick to it, the Covid-19 virus is doomed.

Friendly fire/cytokine storm

Another important component of our immune system is mediated by specialized human cells, as opposed to the free-floating IgG antibodies, such as the fearsome Natural Killer Cells. These cells and others release chemicals called "cytokines" that ruthlessly sacrifice any Covid-19 infected human cells. Unfortunately, they can overdo it. One cause of death from Covid-19 is a massive release of cytokines that causes so much collateral damage to the human body that it, alone, is fatal. This friendly fire problem is called a "cytokine storm".

Pre-training against spike protein tennis balls

Having IgG antibodies directed against the Covid-19 virus's spike protein, at the earliest opportunity, is critically important. If you have already had Covid-19, your immune system will have already produced these antibodies and the next time you encounter the Covid-19 virus it will get up to speed much faster than 14 days. For this reason, a second infection with Covid-19 is rarely serious. This is what is sometimes called "natural" immunity.

The only problem with natural immunity is that you will have to catch and survive Covid-19 to get it. A better strategy would to make sure IgG antibodies are available in full force the very first time Covid-19 enters your system.

It turns out there are actually two ways to do this. The first is to transfuse IgG antibodies from a patient who has already survived Covid-19. This technique will prevent Covid-19 infection sometimes but supplies are limited, transfusion reactions are possible, and the transfused IgG will disappear with time and require a repeat. It is not a good long-term solution.

This technique of transfusing IgG antibodies that someone else made is more useful for certain diseases you will probably only encounter once, or never, in a lifetime such as tetanus or rabies.

With Covid-19, repeat exposures are pretty much guaranteed and we don't know when they will occur, so something more durable is needed.

The second way is that it is possible to train your immune system to recognize Covid-19 spike proteins (tennis balls) the very first time they appear on the beach in your nose, without the two week delay. The training is done before you ever encounter a real live Covid-19 virus, while you are healthy.

The process of training your immune system to recognize and take on the Covid-19 virus on your first exposure could be called "spike protein training camp". Some people consider this to be cheating because it did not result from an actual Covid-19 virus infection. They are entitled to their opinion but it is the exact same IgG antibody molecules in either case.

You have two choices - train your antibody defenses in advance while you are healthy, or train them while you are sick with the Covid-19 virus running amok amongst your organs. Either way takes the same 14 days and produces the same IgG antibodies.

This idea was originally developed in the late 1700s for a specific virus called "vaccinia", which caused smallpox. Because of this the whole procedure was named "vaccination". The name persists although smallpox has now been completely eradicated from the surface of the Earth. The processes involved in vaccination today are much safer and more effective.

Drugs that look like spike protein baseballs

Another option at this perimeter defense stage might be to invent a drug that the ACE2 receptor's catcher's mitt will also mistakenly snare, blocking itself from catching any spike proteins (or normal baseballs, for that matter) that come around later. Drugs like this already exist. They are approved for other uses such as treating high blood pressure, in the form of ACE inhibitors or ARBS (Angiotensin Receptor Blockers).

There is some evidence these drugs actually do prevent Covid-19 infections. One reason they are not used this way very often is that they may lower your blood pressure too much. Another is that they would have to be regularly swallowed or spritzed up your nose to make sure they were always on guard for a random Covid-19 virus invasion. This would be quite inconvenient compared to training your own immune system to patrol on a 24/7 basis.

Resistance to Tactic 4 (consult the assault plan)

After it penetrates the cell's wall, the Covid-19 virus's genome pauses to review its genetic plan. It has the three main tasks discussed in Chapter 1. First, any enzymes it needs but cannot steal from the human cell must be made (especially replicase). Second, it must subvert the cell's own protein-making machinery into preferentially producing Covid-19 virus proteins. Finally, the Covid-19 virus's genome must be replicated, proofread and prepared for assembly into new Covid-19 viruses.

At the time of publication, there are no particularly good ways to interfere with any of these stages without hurting our normal cells as well. Things would never have gone this far if there had been effective perimeter defense.

Resistance to Tactics 5, 6 and 7 (commandeer supplies, tools and energy; fabricate genomes; fabricate armor and weapons)

The Covid-19 virus's ability to take command over the human cell's existing ribosome factories to create consumable supplies, non-consumable tools (the enzymatic "means of production"), and make more Covid-19 virus particles is how the Covid-19 virus manages to stay so small.

Remdesivir is one drug that interferes with replicase in a number of different viruses. It was already on the shelf and so it was tried on Covid-19. Although it does have some activity against Covid-19, it has not proved particularly useful in practice, for various reasons.

Once again, perimeter defense would have been better. The virus is already inside the fortress so any weapon targeting the normal human cell enzymes that the Covid-19 virus has commandeered would likely cause massive collateral damage against all human cells, infected or not. Any drug intended for this stage would also need to be timed correctly, which is much more difficult than training antibodies to be constantly on patrol.[1]

Resistance to Tactics 8 and 9 (muster and break out)

These processes partly depend on specific protein enablers. Some are our own normal cell constituents so attacking them with a drug might again not be tolerated by our healthy cells. There are currently no really useful drugs of this type. The reason none of these tactics that occur inside the cell can be countered with an antibody is that antibodies cannot get inside.

Resistance to Tactic 10 (resume patrol)

The new generation of Covid-19 viruses is by now back on your nasal beach and waiting for its first sortie. Air transport is ideal, either by triggering a sneeze or cough or by patiently waiting for the human to talk, laugh or sing. One form of resistance to this Covid-19 virus tactic would be to inhibit sneezing and coughing with readily available drugs like antihistamines and decongestants.

Another would be to force any exhaled droplets and aerosols to run a gauntlet of tiny holes and electrostatic traps near the source. The same filter material used to protect against inhaling other people's aerosols can also be used to filter your own exhaled air. The catch is that this time it depends on other people, not on you. If they choose to not filter their exhaled air, you will be at risk.

Isolating a known or possibly infected person would also prevent their exhaled droplets and aerosols from getting to you, but it raises issues of freedom. There is nothing new about this idea - it was used in Renaissance Italy for sailors arriving from certain countries, who were required to ride at anchor for 40 days and then supply proof that no one had come down with plague. This period of *quaranta giorni* led to the word quarantine.[2]

For quarantine to be more usefully targeted, it would be essential to know exactly who is infected and who is not, on a daily basis. Waiting for symptoms to appear is inadequate as many victims spread the Covid-19 virus in the days before symptoms start, or never get symptoms at all. Daily testing would certainly help target quarantines but is not generally available.

Quarantine imposes significant personal and societal burdens and would be actively resisted by many. Stricter regulations might just cause people to conceal their symptoms or test results.

---

1. Taking a drug continuously to prevent infection, every day, is not a good option as it would eventually create drug-resistant mutant Covid-19 viruses, by random mutation and natural selection.
2. Italian for "forty days."

CHAPTER 4

COVID-19'S LONG-TERM STRATEGIES

> Science does not aim at establishing immutable truths and eternal dogmas; its aim is to approach the truth by successive approximations, without claiming that at any stage final and complete accuracy has been achieved.
>
> Bertrand Russell

In addition to the specific tactics of a successful invasion and colonization of a human cell, Covid-19 has some longer-term, intergenerational strategies.

Summary

The Covid-19 virus will try to stay ahead of the game by evolving into forms that are more infectious and resist current treatments. This occurs by relentless mutation and natural selection. The more Covid-19 viruses there are, the higher the risk. The world burden of Covid-19 viruses is huge, so this risk is substantial.

Strategy 1: Make the victim work for you

The Covid-19 virus is diabolical in the way it can spread victim to victim without being detected, called asymptomatic spread. This is different from influenza viruses that mostly spread from obviously sick individuals. Worse, the Covid-19 virus can even avoid causing any symptoms at all, yet live and spread until the immune system eventually comes for it 14 days later (discussed below).

Two previous coronaviruses made the leap from animals to humans - the 2003 SARS virus and the 2012 MERS virus.[1] Neither became a pandemic. Part of the reason for this was excellent contact tracing and a diligent public health response but another big reason was that they took down their victims quickly, making them so sick that they could not continue circulating with other humans.

By silently moving around in droplets and aerosols, Covid-19 manages to keep its infiltration activities under the radar.

Strategy 2: Update weapons

The process of copying the Covid-19 virus's genome into millions of new copies is error-prone. An error in the genetic code usually leads to a protein that is the wrong shape and does not work properly. Most such errors are fatal to the Covid-19 virus. To avoid this, Covid-19 viruses have "proofreading enzymes" that find and correct errors as they occur, like a spellchecker. Some errors slip through, giving rise to mutants.

Most of the mutants die, but some can breed and spread. If a mutant happens to spread faster, or be more resistant to our immune system or our drugs, it can outcompete the original Covid-19 virus from which it sprang. After a few generations, more and more of the Covid-19 viruses out on patrol will be mutants. Eventually, they can crowd out all the original Covid-19 viruses. This process is natural selection, the "survival of the fittest", as discussed earlier. At the time of publication, it has brought us the Delta variant. Something worse may be yet to come (see Chapter 19).

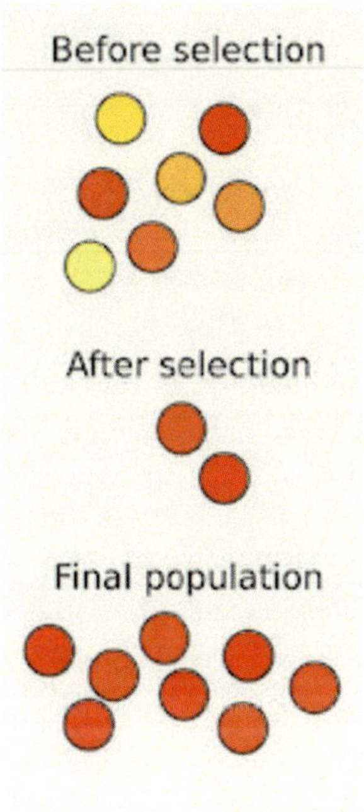

Natural selection of a possible future mutant. Top: seven Covid-19 viruses infect a human, of which two (red) are mutants resistant to all vaccines; Middle: only the red ones survive the human's IgG antibodies that are looking for yellow and orange Covid-19 viruses. Bottom: all the offspring Covid-19 viruses from that particular human are now red.

The animal suspected of harboring the original mutant that "jumped" to humans was probably either a pangolin or a bat. Only a minor change in the genetic code was needed to make one of their coronaviruses thrive in humans, because the pangolin coronavirus's genome was already over 90% the same as Covid-19 and the bat's coronavirus was over 96% the same.[2]

Mutations occur regularly and natural selection does the rest. The best defense is to have an absolute minimum of Covid-19 viruses in the world. The fewer the replicating Covid-19 viruses, the fewer the mutants. Eliminating them in one country but not all countries means huge numbers would still be living and mutating at will, with some spreading worldwide.

Strategy 3: Counter new human defenses

Humans that survive the Covid-19 virus have successfully produced IgG antibodies against the Covid-19 spike protein "tennis ball", which would otherwise trick more and more ACE2 receptors (catcher's mitts) into catching them. These IgG antibodies are like pitcher's mitts - while not exactly the same as the ACE2 catcher's mitts, they are still able to catch Covid-19's spike protein tennis balls.

Evading these IgG antibody pitcher's mitts is high on the list of Covid-19's priorities. Eventually, it may evolve a new spike protein that, for example, looks like a football that the ACE2 receptor (catcher's mitt) can still catch but the IgG antibody (pitcher's mitt) cannot. This would be a disaster. If the pandemic continues to produce millions of daily mutations, the day this happens may not be far off and we will all be back to square one.

Humans have another defense beyond antibodies - we are intelligent and can invent drugs. If we manage to create a really effective Covid-19 drug, will mutation and natural selection eventually just lead to drug-resistant variants? This is certainly a risk and is how drug-resistant bacteria evolved - they were random mutations that turned out to survive exposure to antibiotics, with natural selection promoting them to become successful bacteria in their own right.

---

1. SARS is Severe Acute Respiratory Syndrome; MERS is Middle East Respiratory Syndrome.
2. During the SARS crisis of 2003, the civet cat's coronavirus was over 99% the same as the future human SARS coronavirus.

CHAPTER 5

HOW TO RESIST COVID-19'S STRATEGIES

> MOST PEOPLE WOULD SOONER DIE THAN THINK; IN FACT, THEY DO SO.
>
> BERTRAND RUSSELL

Summary

Filtering exhaled air and killing Covid-19 wherever it shows up, in any part of the world, will resist its longer-term strategies.

Resistance to Strategy 1 (make the victim work for you)

To accomplish this goal, the Covid-19 virus keeps the victim asymptomatic and surreptitiously spreading Covid-19 viruses by normal talking, heavy breathing during exercise, etc. The most effective resistance to this strategy would be to talk and breathe through filters, as discussed above concerning coughs and sneezes. There is no substitute for not letting Covid-19 loose in the first place.

Nasal irrigation might also help keep the number of Covid-19 viruses waiting on the "beach" down by washing them away in the tide. For various reasons, this is not likely to be very effective.

Aerosolization of Covid-19 viruses in tiny bubbles is more efficient at higher body temperatures, so treating a fever with standard medications is probably also reasonable.

Resistance to Strategies 2 and 3 (update weapons and counter new defenses)

Both of these Covid-19 virus strategies depend on random mutation and natural selection. This means Covid-19 needs to exist in massive numbers, which generate large numbers of mutants, which result in occasional viable strains with advantages, which sometimes end up in a human nose. This is presumably how the Delta and other variants came about. There will likely be others as long as the pool of Covid-19 viruses in the world remains as large as it is now.

Mutants arising in faraway countries will soon find you, even if you are in Antarctica. The best way to reduce this risk is to attack and eliminate Covid-19 viruses wherever they occur.

Fewer Covid-19 viruses means fewer mutants. Besides being the ethical thing to do it is in every developed country's enlightened self-interest to eliminate Covid-19 in poorer countries, everywhere in the world.

Summary of resistance options for all Covid-19 tactics and strategies

TACTIC 1: resist Covid-19 viruses out on patrol and looking for you by keeping your distance and filtering the air you inhale;

TACTICS 2 AND 3: resist Covid-19 viruses after they land in your nose but before they enter a nose cell, by advance training your IgG antibodies against the Covid-19 spike protein so they are fully armed when they first encounter a Covid-19 virus;

Tactics 4-9: there are no really good defenses available, largely because Covid-19 is now inside and using your cell's own metabolism - you cannot poison it without poisoning yourself;

Tactic 10: make it harder for Covid-19 to leave you on patrol for a new victim by filtering your coughs and sneezes, and by using decongestants or antihistamines;

Strategy 1: prevent Covid-19 floating to nearby people in your droplets or aerosols by filtering the air you expire during normal breathing and talking;

Strategies 2 and 3: minimize mutations by reducing the pool of Covid-19 viruses worldwide.

CHAPTER 6

WHAT EXACTLY IS A VACCINE?

> THE WHOLE PROBLEM WITH THE WORLD IS THAT FOOLS AND FANATICS ARE ALWAYS SO CERTAIN OF THEMSELVES, AND WISER PEOPLE SO FULL OF DOUBTS.
>
> BERTRAND RUSSELL

There are many types of vaccine. They should all be judged by the same standard - are they less risky and dangerous than the disease itself? Vaccines do not need to be perfect or completely free of risk, they just need to be better than all other options.

Summary

The way to make our immune system react faster to its very first encounter with live Covid-19 virus is to pre-train it against spike protein. There are several ways to do this effectively and safely.

How vaccines work

Vaccines have eradicated or drastically reduced many viral and bacterial diseases from North America including smallpox, poliomyelitis, rubella, mumps, anthrax, rabies, tetanus and diphtheria. Other diseases have so far proved impossible to eliminate, notably syphilis.[1] The importance of vaccination is sometimes not fully appreciated by people who were born after the 1930s.

Immunity is all about having IgG antibodies trained as sentries on patrol, 24/7. Our immune system takes 14 days to train these guards. Once available, they appear in the form of IgG antibodies (pitcher's mitts) and are wonderfully effective at sticking to and inactivating the Covid-19 virus spike proteins (tennis balls).

If you do not have pre-trained IgG antibodies and you are unlucky, the Covid-19 virus will run wild in your body for 14 days. By the time they appear you might be very sick or even dead.

Once it has been trained to recognize the Covid-19 virus's spike protein the first time the immune system will react faster the next time. Assuming you survived the first bout, the next Covid-19 to appear on your nasal beach will be immediately nuked.

So can we convince the immune system to climb that 14-day learning curve before the first infection, so it is ready? It is possible if we prime it with spike protein ahead of time, when you are well.

There are several different ways to do this, at least in principle. The actual Covid-19 vaccines that have resulted from a few of these techniques will be discussed in Chapter 7.

Option 1: using a live virus related to Covid-19

In 1796, Edward Jenner injected a boy with live cowpox viruses from a milkmaid's hands (milkmaids all had cowpox). Later, he injected the same boy with live smallpox viruses. The boy did not get small pox. This experiment was unethical, of course, and nothing similar would ever be attempted today. It did, at least, prove that the immune system can be pre-trained. The procedure was called vaccination, in reference to the defeated vaccinia virus. If a vaccine could be made that was less of a risk than the actual disease in question, it might prove useful.

Option 2: using a dead Covid-19 virus

Viruses that are cooked just long enough to kill them, but that still brandish an important surface protein (like Covid-19's spike protein), could be injected. Antibodies against the surface protein may be formed. The Salk polio vaccine and most current influenza vaccines work this way.

Option 3: using a weakened Covid-19 virus

In this approach, Covid-19 could be weakened in the lab so that it is just barely able to survive inside cells but not enough to cause symptoms or disease. All the weakened virus would be able to do is listlessly sit inside your cell producing spike protein, which then trains your immune system. The weakened Covid-19 virus would not be able to actually make you sick, at least in theory. The measles vaccine works this way.

Option 4: spike protein from a harmless adenovirus

Adenovirus is a common human virus that commonly causes colds. Some laboratory-created strains are not able to cause disease but can still be used for their ability to enter human cells. If they are made to carry the Covid-19 virus's gene for spike protein, it will enter the cell, too. If it then produces the mRNA for spike protein, the spike protein will be manufactured by the human cell's ribosomal protein factory and the immune system will be pre-trained against it. This approach was used for the successful 2019 Ebola vaccine.

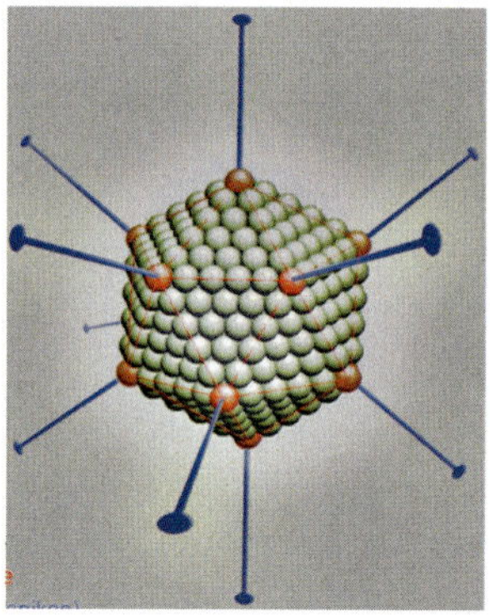

A non-viable adenovirus containing the Covid-19 spike protein gene manages to enter a human cell and bring the Covid-19 spike protein gene with it. It produces spike protein but cannot replicate into more adenoviruses.

Option 5: using pure spike protein

Purified Covid-19 spike protein could be injected, similar to the existing vaccine for hepatitis B. It would then stimulate the immune system to produce IgG antibodies abasing spike protein.

Option 6: inserting the spike protein gene into the human genome

This approach would tinker with our genetic code and is considered too risky.

Option 7: messenger RNA

Messenger RNA (mRNA), the blueprint that takes instructions from your genes to your ribosomal protein factory, can be made in the laboratory. It is possible to sneak the mRNA molecules into human cells in a tiny oil drop. Once inside, the mRNA plays its usual role. If it is mRNA coding for Covid-19 spike protein, for example, the cell produces Covid-19 spike protein - no infection or viruses of any kind needed.

This technique is very modern, demanding and clean. It would not require any human genes, Covid-19 genes or adenovirus genes, just the mRNA blueprint for one specific protein (the Covid-19 spike protein).

Other options

An alternative vaccine that is spritzed up the nose, instead of being injected, has now been abandoned by Altimmune.

Snorting pure spike protein into the nose is under investigation. Spike protein given orally would just be digested as food.

Squirting IgG antibodies into the nose might work but would probably need to be repeated several times a day. Unfortunately, even if it worked it would not cause our immune system to generate its own IgG antibodies against Covid-19 spike protein so there would be no 24/7 protection unless repeated frequently.

India is currently developing a plasmid-based vaccine; however, this is beyond the scope of this book.

---

1. Neurosyphilis was the main cause of adult neurological hospitalizations prior to the development of antibiotics in the twentieth century. Historically, the Dutch called syphilis the Spanish disease, the French called it the Neapolitan disease, the Germans, English and Italians called it the French disease, the Turks called it the Christian disease, the Hindus called it the Muslim disease and the Muslims (in India) called it the Hindu disease.

CHAPTER 7

VACCINES FOR COVID-19

I WOULD NEVER DIE FOR MY BELIEFS, BECAUSE I MIGHT BE WRONG.

BERTRAND RUSSELL

Two of these types of vaccine have been studied carefully and have the potential to be better than the alternatives, which include getting Covid-19. These will be described here, with the benefits and risks fully assessed in Chapters 9 - 14.

Summary

Messenger RNA (mRNA) vaccines and adenovirus vaccines are available in the US, Canada and elsewhere.

Messenger RNA (mRNA) vaccines

The US and Canada have each approved two mRNA vaccines. These are the Pfizer-BioNTech and Moderna vaccines.

The main disadvantages of mRNA vaccines is they need to be transported and handled at very cold temperatures, and require second or even third injections (boosters). The main advantage is that they are clean and there is very little potential for side effects.

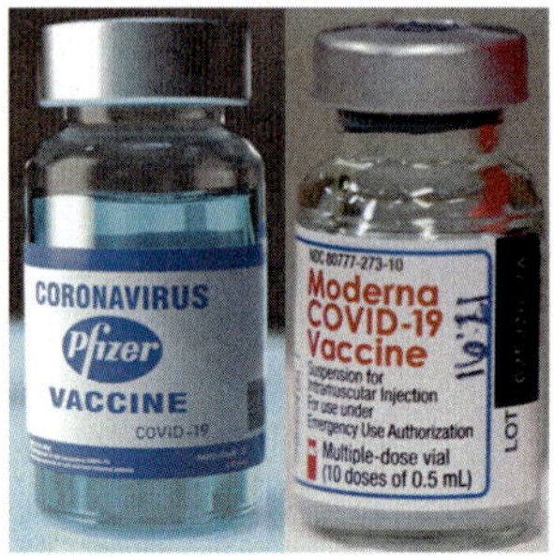

The Pfizer and Moderna mRNA vaccines.

Adenovirus vaccines

The US has approved the Johnson & Johnson (Janssen) vaccine. Canada has approved both Johnson & Johnson and the Oxford-AstraZeneca vaccine. A version of the AstraZeneca vaccine that is made in India, CoviShield, is also available in Canada.

The main problem with AstraZeneca is that it needs two injections; however, handling is easier than for mRNA vaccines. Johnson & Johnson is also easy to handle and needs only a single injection.

Although the Johnson & Johnson vaccine is approved in Canada, it is not actually used there. The first order had to be canceled due to manufacturing defects and no one was interested after that. The Sputnik vaccine in Russia is also adenovirus-based but not used in North America.

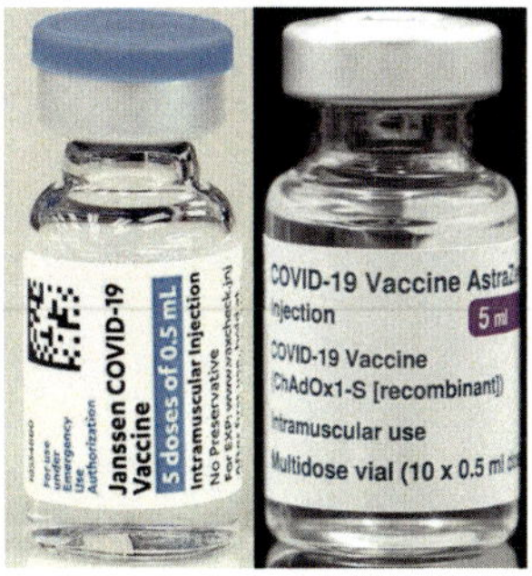

The Johnson & Johnson and AstraZeneca adenovirus vaccines.

Other vaccines

Dead Covid-19 vaccines

The Sinopharm (China), CoronaVac (China) and Covaxin (India) vaccines are all dead ("inactivated") Covid-19 virus. They are not approved in the US or Canada.

Pure spike protein vaccines

China produces a pure spike protein vaccine called ZF2001. The US has produced a similar vaccine called Novavax. Neither is approved in the US or Canada.

DNA plasmid vaccines

Plasmid vaccines are not available yet and are beyond the scope of this book.

CHAPTER 8

HOW TO COMPARE BENEFITS AND RISKS

IF AN OPINION CONTRARY TO YOUR OWN MAKES YOU ANGRY, THAT IS A SIGN THAT YOU ARE SUBCONSCIOUSLY AWARE OF HAVING NO GOOD REASON FOR THINKING AS YOU DO.

BERTRAND RUSSELL

Chapters 9-14 involve numbers at approximately a Grade 6 level. This is unavoidable as there are not enough words in English to convey the various facts and probabilities any other way. Math is just a way of thinking clearly.

Doctors make decisions about medical or surgical treatments based on a comparison of the benefits and risks, and so should you. This is not an exact science as the risks mean different things to different people, but it is a start. Provided that all benefits and risks important to you are included in the analysis, a benefit-to-risk ratio of more than one means you should at least consider the treatment, and less than one means you should consider forgoing the treatment. The further this number is away from one, the stronger the conclusion. For example, two-to-one odds would not be as persuasive as million-to-one odds.

Chapters 9-13 are an attempt to define the benefit-to-risk ratio for the specific issue of being vaccinated versus not being vaccinated. This is probably the single most important question to readers of this book. The "benefit" of a vaccine is defined here as the risk of death from Covid-19 that can be avoided by vaccination, as a number. The "risk" of a vaccine is defined here as the probability of serious adverse effects or death due to the vaccine, as a number. The "benefit-to-risk ratio" is then the benefit divided by the risk.

This initial analysis still leaves out some potentially important details. For example, when considering the benefits it does not include the value of avoiding aspects of severe Covid-19 that do not result in actual death, such as intense suffering, financial loss, infecting your family, etc. These are considered further in Chapter 14.

On the risk side, this analysis does not account for minor side effects. No attempt has been made to account for these here due to the difficulty of finding any reasonable scale that would include death at one end and a one-day sore arm at the other. If you are able to quantify the importance of minor side effects to you, please add them to the risks and recalculate.

CHAPTER 9

BASIC COVID-19 STATISTICS

To understand the actual world as it is, not as we should wish it to be, is the beginning of wisdom.

Bertrand Russell

Once again, we need to understand exactly who or what the enemy is before planning how to defeat it. The pandemic has lasted 1.5 years so far, long enough to have good data on its risks and mortality. We will use this data to predict how the next 1.5 years might unfold.

Summary

- The risk of a healthy person catching AND dying of Covid-19 in the US is 0.19% per 1.5 years;
- The risk of a healthy person catching AND dying of Covid-19 in Canada is 0.07% per 1.5 years.

Details

United States

- The US population is 332,000,000;
- Over the last 1.5 years, 39,700,000 people have contracted Covid-19, amounting to 12% of the population;
- Over the last 1.5 years, 645,000 of the people with Covid-19 have died, amounting to 1.6% of the infected people;
- The risk of an otherwise normal person catching AND then dying of Covid-19 has therefore been about 12% x 1.6%, or about 0.19%. This will be our estimate for the future.

Canada

- The population of Canada is 38,000,000.
- Over the last 1.5 years, 1,500,000 people have contracted Covid-19, amounting to 3.9% of the population;
- Over the last 1.5 years, 27,000 of the people with Covid-19 have died, amounting to 1.8% of the infected people;
- The risk of an otherwise normal person catching AND then dying of Covid-19 has therefore been about 3.9% x 1.8%, or about 0.07%. This will be our estimate for the future.

ICU beds and ventilators

These figures might appear to be small numbers; however, they are not. If you live in an average US city of 50,000 people, then the 0.19% of the population lost over the past 1.5 years is about 100 people. There have been four big waves of infection during that 1.5 years, which is about 25 deaths per wave. If most of these people died in hospital on ventilators, that means your local hospital would need about 25 ventilator beds. An "ICU bed" means a physical bed, a room to put it in, a ventilator, ancillary equipment, at least two intravenous lines for fluids, tube feeding apparatus, medication administration lines, suction apparatus, catheter drainage, an oxygen monitor, a blood pressure monitor, a heart rhythm monitor, and at least two highly trained ICU nurses to take turns providing you with one-to-one care. This is very hard to come up with if the hospital does not already have it. As medical and nursing personnel "burn out" and leave, it will only get worse.

The average number of ICU beds in a US city of 50,000 is actually only 13, so if the above 25 people need it at the same time, clearly half will not get it. If you are one of them in respiratory failure with no available ventilator, you will likely gasp for breath for hours to days, then die. In normal times, you could possibly be sent to another city, but if they are also coping with a Covid-19 wave this won't be possible.

The corresponding number for Canada is even more dismal, with only 6.5 ICU beds available per city of 50,000 people.

Clearly, an average city in either country cannot cope with this. To be safe, you should either arrange to get Covid-19 between infection waves, or to not get it at all.

If you are from a smaller city in either country, there may be no ICU at all.

Urban versus rural risks

If you live in a rural area, it is true that your risk of catching Covid-19 is less that the average. On the other hand, the chance of dying if you do catch it is probably higher. As a result, your chances of catching AND dying of Covid-19 are not that much different from the average for your country and the numerical arguments discussed below apply to you, too.

Comments

Once you have already contracted Covid-19, the chance of dying in the United States and Canada is similar, due to similar hospital care (1.6% and 1.8%, respectively).

The chance of catching AND dying of Covid-19 in the United States is almost three times that in Canada (0.19% compared to 0.07% in Canada), even though Canada has fewer ICU beds per 50,000 people. This appears to be at least partly due to different attitudes towards public health measures and vaccination.

CHAPTER 10

COVID-19 VACCINE BENEFITS

SCIENCE DOES NOT AIM AT ESTABLISHING IMMUTABLE TRUTHS AND ETERNAL DOGMAS; ITS AIM IS TO APPROACH THE TRUTH BY SUCCESSIVE APPROXIMATIONS, WITHOUT CLAIMING THAT AT ANY STAGE FINAL AND COMPLETE ACCURACY HAS BEEN ACHIEVED.

BERTRAND RUSSELL

The "benefit" of a vaccine is defined here as the risk of death we hope it nullifies. The benefit would be high in a crowded third world city like Dacca, and less in Antarctica.

Summary

The "benefit" of the various vaccines, corrected for their efficacies, are:

- Pfizer and Moderna in the US: 0.18%
- Pfizer or Moderna in Canada: 0.07%

- Johnson & Johnson in the US: 0.17%
- AstraZeneca in Canada: 0.07%

Details

From the last chapter, the risks of a healthy person catching AND dying of Covid in the US or Canada as a whole were:

- United States: 0.19%
- Canada: 0.07%

However, the vaccines are not 100% effective. Their "efficacies" are:

- Pfizer and Moderna: 95%
- Johnson & Johnson: 85%
- AstraZeneca: 100%

Correcting for these efficacies, the actual benefits are as follows:

United States

- Pfizer and Moderna: 95% x 0.19%, which is 0.18%;
- Johnson & Johnson: 85% x 0.19%, which is 0.17%

Canada

- Pfizer and Moderna: 95% x 0.07%, which is 0.07%;
- AstraZeneca: 100% x 0.07%, which is 0.07%.

Comment

The reason the vaccines are of less benefit in Canada than the US is that the risk of catching Covid-19 in Canada is lower.

CHAPTER 11

COVID-19 VACCINE RISKS

The fact that an opinion has been widely held is no evidence whatever that it is not utterly absurd.

Bertrand Russell

The "risk" of a vaccine is defined here as the chance of serious adverse effects, including death.

Summary

The risks of the vaccines are:

- Pfizer and Moderna mRNA vaccines: 0.000002%.
- Johnson & Johnson adenovirus vaccine: 0.0008%.
- AstraZeneca adenovirus vaccine: 0.003%.

Details

Major adverse effects with Pfizer and Moderna mRNA vaccines in the US or Canada

- The two mRNA vaccines, Pfizer and Moderna, have so far been associated with 0 deaths, 3 heart attacks and 3 strokes. There have been no cases of VITT, CVST or GBS;[1]
- A total of 350,000,000 doses have been injected;
- If the 6 heart attacks and strokes are attributed to the vaccines, then the risk of major adverse effects or death is 6 divided by 350,000,000, which is 0.000002%.

Major adverse effects with Johnson & Johnson adenovirus vaccine in the US

- In the US, 6 cases of VITT or CVST have occurred. Guillain-Barré syndrome has occurred in about 100 patients, for a total of 106 major adverse effects;
- A total of 13,000,000 doses have been injected;
- The combined risk of any of these three problems occurring is therefore 106 divided by 13,000,000 sum, or about 0.0008%.

Major adverse effects with AstraZeneca adenovirus vaccine in Canada

- In Canada, CVST has occurred in 40 patients (fatal in 5). VITT has occurred in 28, for a total of 68 major adverse effects;
- A total of 2,000,000 doses have been given;

- This means the risk of either complication in Canada, fatal or not, is about 0.003%.[2]

Minor side effects of vaccines

Most vaccines can cause minor side effects such as pain at the injection site. The needle itself, regardless of what is injected, can also cause local tissue trauma and bleeding. These side effects are insignificant in the overall picture and will not be discussed further.

Myocarditis and pericarditis are inflammation of the heart muscle and the pericardium, respectively. Over a million cases have been reported following mRNA vaccinations (Pfizer and Moderna) but so far it appears the vast majority recover completely, so it is considered here as a minor side effect pending further information.

Comments

Sometimes adverse effects occur purely by chance. For example, although 0.6% of adults vaccinated with Pfizer reported a minor side effect, so did 0.5% of the control group who did not receive the vaccine.

Some have argued that the risk of blood clots (such as CVST or VITT) is even higher in patients with severe Covid-19 than in healthy people after a vaccination. This is true, but it is comparing apples and oranges if we are trying to answer the question about the risks to currently healthy people (as opposed to Covid-19 patients) being vaccinated.

---

1. VITT: Vaccine-Induced Thrombocytopenic Thrombosis can cause blood clots anywhere, with the potential to move (embolize) to the lungs, and death from various causes. Also called TTS (Thrombosis with Thrombocytopenia Syndrome).

   CVST: Cerebral Venous Sinus Thrombosis (CVST) causes blood clots in the brain, potentially leading to strokes and/or death.

GBS: In Guillain-Barré syndrome, the body's nerves stop working although the brain and spinal cord continue to function. At its worst, all muscles are paralyzed, including those needed for breathing. It may require artificial ventilation for weeks to months.

2. This is comparable to AstraZeneca in Britain, where the risk has been estimated at 1 in 50,000, or 0.002%.

CHAPTER 12

WHAT ARE MY ODDS?

IN ALL AFFAIRS IT'S A HEALTHY THING NOW AND THEN TO HANG A QUESTION MARK ON THE THINGS YOU HAVE LONG TAKEN FOR GRANTED.

BERTRAND RUSSELL

The previous two chapters have derived the benefit and risk for each vaccine. ." Place your bet wisely.

Summary

Any vaccine with a benefit-to-risk ratio over 1 is better to take than to not take. All available vaccines in Canada and the US are in this category. While any vaccine is better than no vaccine, an mRNA vaccine is safer.

The key question

The choice a vaccine-hesitant person faces is:

Should I take my chances on not being vaccinated, knowing that I could get very sick or die of Covid-19?

OR

Should I take my chances on being vaccinated, knowing that I could get very sick or die from the vaccination?

The benefit-to-risk ratio

United States, Pfizer or Moderna

- The benefit of Pfizer or Moderna is 0.18%;
- The risk of Pfizer or Moderna is 0.000002%;
- The benefit-to-risk ratio is therefore 0.18% ÷ 0.000002%, which is 92,282;
- An average healthy person is therefore over 90,000 times better off to be vaccinated with ~~Johnson & Johnson~~ than if not vaccinated at all. Pfizer or Moderna

United States, Johnson & Johnson

- The benefit of Johnson & Johnson is 0.17%;
- The risk of Johnson & Johnson is 0.0008%;
- The benefit-to-risk ratio is therefore 0.17% ÷ 0.0008%, which is 206;
- An average healthy person is therefore over 200 times better off to be vaccinated with Johnson & Johnson than to be not vaccinated at all.

Canada, Pfizer or Moderna

- The benefit of Pfizer or Moderna is 0.07%;
- The risk of Pfizer or Moderna is 0.000002%;
- The benefit-to-risk ratio is therefore 0.07% ÷ 0.000002%, which is 33,750;
- An average healthy person is therefore over 30,000 times better off to be vaccinated with Pfizer or Moderna than to be not vaccinated at all.

Canada, AstraZeneca

- The benefit of AstraZeneca is 0.07%;
- The risk of AstraZeneca is 0.003%;
- The benefit-to-risk ratio is therefore 0.07% ÷ 0.003%, which is 24;
- An average healthy person is therefore over 20 times better off to be vaccinated with AstraZeneca than to be not vaccinated at all.

Comments

1. We compared the risk of death (only) from Covid-19 with the risk of death OR serious adverse effects with each vaccine. That was done intentionally to weigh the scales against vaccination, for the sake of credibility. Even so, it turned out that any of the vaccines are better than no vaccine.

2. The reason the Pfizer and Moderna odds are even more in favour of vaccination in the US than Canada is that the "benefit" is higher in the US, because the risk of dying of Covid-19 is higher.

3. To compare these benefits and risks with other well-known small numbers, consider lotteries. Many people, the author included, think a lottery ticket is worthwhile because there is the possibility of a huge win for almost no cost.

In the US, your chance of winning the "Covid-19 lottery" **without vaccination** is the same as the chance of not dying of Covid-19 over the next 1.5 years, which is 0.9981.[1] The chance of winning the Lucky for Life lottery is 0.00000003.[2] These both look small, but you would be over 60 thousand times better off with the vaccination than the lottery ticket.[3]

In Canada, your chance of winning the "Covid-19 lottery" **without vaccination** is the chance of not dying of Covid-19 over the next 1.5 years, which is 0.9993.[4] The chance of winning the 6/49 lottery is 0.00000007.[5] These both look small, but you would be 10 thousand times better off with the vaccination than the lottery ticket.[6]

---

1. 1.0000 - 0.0019.
2. 1 ÷ 30,821,472.
3. 0.0019 ÷ 0.00000003, which is 33,270,000.
4. 1.0000 - 0.0007.
5. 1 ÷ 13,983,816.
6. 0.0007 ÷ 0.00000007, which is 10,000.

CHAPTER 13

A REVIEW OF THE NUMBERS

MAN IS A CREDULOUS ANIMAL, AND MUST BELIEVE SOMETHING; IN THE ABSENCE OF GOOD GROUNDS FOR BELIEF, HE WILL BE SATISFIED WITH BAD ONES.

BERTRAND RUSSELL

The two tables below summarize the numerical arguments of Chapters 9 - 13, for the United States and for Canada.

United States

Line		Pfizer or Moderna mRNA	J&J adenovirus
1	**Population of the United States**	332,000,000	332,000,000
2	**Total Covid cases in first 1.5 years**	39,700,000	39,700,000
3	**Risk of catching Covid-19 in first 1.5 years**	12.0%	12.0%
4	**Total Covid deaths in first 1.5 years**	645,000	645,000
5	**Risk of death if you have Covid-19 in first 1.5 years**	1.6%	1.6%
6	**Risk and catching AND dying of Covid-19, next 1.5 years**	0.19%	0.19%
7	**Vaccine efficacy in preventing severe Covid-19**	95%	85%
8	**Adjusted benefit, next 1.5 years**	0.18%	0.17%
9	**Risk of vaccine**	0.000002%	0.0009%
10	**Odds favoring vaccination over next 1.5 years**	92,282	183

Lines 1, 2 and 4 are basic demographic data;

Lines 7 and 9 are clinical data.

Line 3 is Line 2 ÷ Line 1;

Line 5 is Line 4 ÷ Line 2;

Line 6 is Line 3 x Line 5;

Line 8 Line 6 x Line 7;

Line 10 is Line 8 ÷ Line 9.

Canada

Line		Pfizer or Moderna mRNA	AstraZeneca adenovirus
1	**Population of Canada**	38,000,000	38,000,000
2	**Total Covid cases in first 1.5 years**	1,500,000	1,500,000
3	**Risk of catching Covid-19 in first 1.5 years**	3.9%	3.9%
4	**Total Covid deaths in first 1.5 years**	27,000	27,000
5	**Risk of death if you have Covid-19 in first 1.5 years**	1.8%	1.8%
6	**Risk and catching AND dying of Covid-19, next 1.5 years**	0.07%	0.07%
7	**Vaccine efficacy in preventing severe Covid-19**	95%	100%
8	**Adjusted benefit, next 1.5 years**	0.07%	0.07%
9	**Risk of vaccine**	0.000002%	0.005%
10	**Odds favoring vaccination over next 1.5 years**	33,750	14

Lines 1, 2 and 4 are basic demographic data;

Lines 7 and 9 are clinical data.

Line 3 is Line 2 ÷ Line 1;

Line 5 is Line 4 ÷ Line 2;

Line 6 is Line 3 x Line 5;

Line 8 Line 6 x Line 7;

Line 10 is Line 8 ÷ Line 9.

CHAPTER 14

WORSE THAN DEATH?

If a man is offered a fact which goes against his instincts, he will scrutinize it closely, and unless the evidence is overwhelming, he will refuse to believe it. If, on the other hand, he is offered something which affords a reason for acting in accordance to his instincts, he will accept it even on the slightest evidence.

Bertrand Russell

Chapter 12 and 13 considered the odds in favour of a good result, expressed as the benefit-to-risk ratio, based on simple numbers. In doing so, we considered the only bad outcome of having Covid-19 to be death. But death is only part of the story. This chapter considers other issues.

Summary

Besides death, other unpleasant things about Covid-19 include the manner of death, infecting your family, loss of earnings, the cost of medical care (in the US), etc. If these factors are weighted into the benefit-to-risk ratios, vaccination is the preferred strategy by a factor of up to one trillion to one. The mRNA vaccines remain safer than the adenovirus vaccines, but any available vaccine is much safer than not being vaccinated.

What is worse than death?

What is worse than being dead? For one thing, the Covid-19 style of dying is not very pleasant. Imagine two to three weeks of suffocating and gasping for every breath, then dying. If you think this might be twice as bad as a sudden painless death, for example, then multiply the benefit-to-risk ratio by 2.

Multiply by another factor of 2 for every other possibility that would make things even worse. Examples might include infecting your family members, infecting strangers, the cost of medical care (in the US) or financial stress from prolonged illness. If all four are a concern, multiply by 2 four more times.

That is still not all. If you are pregnant and want to avoid possible oxygen problems for the baby while you are gradually succumbing on your ventilator, another factor of 2 is reasonable.

You might also be left with long-term illness, which is especially important if you already have any chronic illnesses. If you think it would be a good idea to avoid this risk, another factor of 2 would apply.

If every one of the above strikes you as a good reason to avoid getting Covid-19, that is **seven factors of 2** (which is 128). The benefit-to-risk ratios now look like this:

Benefit-to-risk ratios with seven factors of two

- United States with Pfizer or Moderna: the odds ratio is now 92,282 x 128, which is 11,812,096;
- United States with Johnson & Johnson: the odds ratio is 206 x 128, which is 26,368.

- Canada with Pfizer or Moderna: the odds ratio is 33,750 x 128, which is 4,320,000;
- Canada with AstraZeneca: the odds ratio is 24 x 128, which is 3,072.

Benefit-to-risk ratios with seven factors of ten

The above figures assumed each factor made your potential experience with Covid-19 twice as bad. That number was chosen so as not to exaggerate. However, in the opinion of many Covid-19 survivors (and the author), a figure of **ten times worse** would be more realistic. If this were used instead, the resulting benefit-to-risk ratios would be:

- United States with Pfizer or Moderna: the odds ratio is now 92,282 x 10,000,000, which is 922,820,000,000;
- United States with Johnson & Johnson: the odds ratio is 206 x 10,000,000, which is 2,060,000,000;

- Canada with Pfizer or Moderna: the odds ratio is 33,750 x 10,000,000, which is 337,500,000,000;
- Canada with AstraZeneca: the odds ratio is 24 x 10,000,000, which is 240,000,000.

CHAPTER 15

TREATMENT OF COVID-19

IT IS THE THINGS FOR WHICH THERE IS NO EVIDENCE THAT ARE BELIEVED WITH PASSION.

BERTRAND RUSSELL

Treatment of established Covid-19 infection depends on what organs are affected and how severely. It can damage multiple organs at once. This section is a brief review. If your own physician disagrees with anything, believe him or her, not this book.

Summary

There are no really good drugs developed specifically for Covid-19. Passive transfusion of IgG antibodies from a survivor and remdesivir are minor players. Various options exist for life support, organ failure and downgrading the immune system's cytokine storm. Any kind of intensive care treatment is likely to be invasive, painful and dangerous compared with not getting Covid-19 at all.

What can go wrong

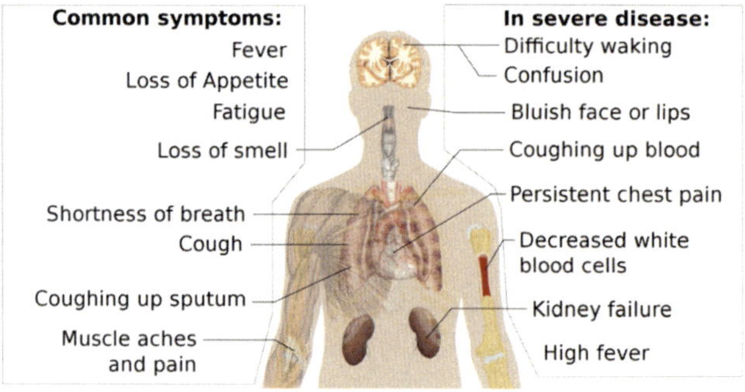

Covid-19 affects every organ system.

Too little oxygen

The worst Covid-19 casualty will probably be your lungs. One of their tasks is to bring blood and inspired air into close contact so that oxygen can diffuse from the air to the blood. The blood is then circulated around the body. If the lung cells do not work properly, or if inflammatory fluids accumulate, oxygen cannot diffuse and body organs begin to fail. This, in turn, will affect all other organs including your brain.

Too much carbon dioxide

The second task of the lungs is to get rid of carbon dioxide, the waste product of metabolism. It needs to diffuse from blood to air, then be exhaled. Our brains monitor carbon dioxide extremely closely and will create the intense feeling of a suffocating shortness of breath if it rises even a little. In normal circumstances a ventilator would relieve much of this. With Covid-19 and everyone getting sick at once, you could remain in this state for days or weeks, until people even worse off than you die and you get their ventilator.

Pneumonia

Your lungs can also stop working when normal bystander bacteria notice you are sick and move in for the kill. The infection can spread to other organs or your blood.

Kidney failure

The kidneys control water and electrolyte balance as well as filtering out toxins. If they stop working, you are looking at a dialysis machine, assuming one is available at the height of an infection wave.

Liver failure

Your liver has many functions essential to life. It, too, can fail and is complex to treat.

Cytokine storm

Cytokine storm, the excessively exuberant release of cytokines by the immune system in the face of overwhelming infection, damages many organ systems. Multiple organ failure is very difficult to manage.

Disseminated Intravascular Coagulation (DIC)

This condition is similar to VITT and CVST (see above), the dreaded complications of adenovirus vaccines that occasionally cause blood clots to form. DIC can be even worse; however. Your blood suddenly clots everywhere, not just in one vein or venous sinus. All body organs shut down at the same time for lack of blood supply. And because this catastrophe just used up all your clotting factors and platelets, you also start bleeding, anywhere.

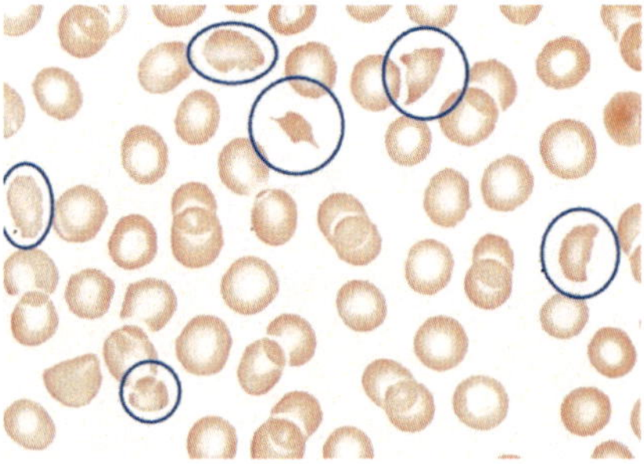

This interesting microscope image shows normal red blood cells and fractured pieces of red blood cells (marked) in a patient with DIC. Even the tiniest blood vessels in this person were so full of clots that tiny red blood cells actually broke into pieces trying to squeeze through them.

Treatment options

Oxygen

Oxygen-enriched air is adequate for less severe cases.

Ventilator

If respiration fails, leading to carbon dioxide buildup and an excessive fall in oxygen levels, a ventilator is required. A tube is inserted in your throat and the machine takes over your breathing. This is unpleasant so you will be sedated and possibly even paralyzed with drugs. Often the lung damage is too severe for even a ventilator to overcome, usually leading to death.

Extracorporeal membrane oxygenation (ECMO)

If the lungs are so diseased that even a ventilator is failing, a form of mechanical lung can be used. Blood is circulated through it and returned to the body. It is complex to use and not generally available, and it has numerous complications, including strokes. One study showed about one-third of patients receiving ECMO had complications such as strokes, and one-third died. Not getting Covid-19 is a much better option.

Fluids, nutrition, kidney dialysis, etc.

The function of other organs such as the kidney and liver can be supported, to a point.

Antibiotics

If bacteria move into your failing body, antibiotics may be required. This is complex as some bacteria are resistant to antibiotics and all antibiotics are potentially toxic. Many infections cannot be treated adequately, leading to death.

Sedation and pain control

Pain and the sense of drowning can be intense and may need powerful drugs to treat; however, sedation can make respiration even worse and has to be used with extreme caution.

Repurposed antiviral drugs

Neuraminidase inhibitors used for influenza, such as oseltamivir, do not work with Covid-19. The HIV protease inhibitors lopinavir and ritonavir also do not work. Remdesivir, a drug active against some RNA viruses, is somewhat useful.

Antibodies against covid-19 spike protein

Blood transfusions (plasma) from patients who built up their own IgG spike protein antibodies and survived Covid-19, also called convalescent plasma, can help temporarily. IgG antibodies to spike protein can also be made in the laboratory and include drugs like bamlanivimab, etesevimab, casirivimab, imdevimab and sotrovimab.

Antibodies work against viruses or molecules that are in the bloodstream. Once a Covid-19 virus has entered the cell it is no longer vulnerable to antibodies. The offspring viruses may again enter the bloodstream and theoretically be susceptible to antibodies again, but in practice you are likely to be so sick by this point that nothing works very well.

Antibodies and drugs against cytokine storm

Steroids, in high doses, are extremely powerful anti-inflammation drugs but come with many serious side effects including stomach ulcers, diabetes, destruction of the hip joint and fractures. If cytokine storm is a problem, high dose steroids may be lifesaving.

Tocilizumab and baricitinib are antibodies against specific cytokines and are used sometimes. Fluvoxamine, technically an antidepressant, has properties, unrelated to its primary purpose that might inhibit cytokine storm; however, it has not proved very useful in practice.

Ineffective treatments

Hydroxychloroquine

Hydroxychloroquine and chloroquine target the parasite causing malaria. At first, some people wondered if it might also be useful with Covid-19 and some even promoted it publicly. Unfortunately, clinical research has shown it to be ineffective.

Disinfectants

Snorting non-specific disinfectants up the nose, such as povidone-iodine, hydrogen peroxide or even detergents, might work locally but would be unpleasant and need frequent applications. It would do nothing for the rest of the body. A recent US president suggested injecting chlorine into the body (in the form of bleach), reasoning that it "does a tremendous number on the lungs". It certainly would, as the Germans understood when they used it as a chemical weapon during World War I.

Ivermectin

This drug was initially promoted in a fraudulent scientific report from Egypt. The author has since admitted the data was false.

While ivermectin does have some weak anti-viral activity in the test tube, as many things do, legitimate clinical research has demonstrated that it does not work for actual humans with Covid-19. Like all drugs, it has side effects. Taking ivermectin obtained from farm stores and intended for deworming animals, is especially risky and can make you very sick. If ivermectin worked this well it would, of course, be used by doctors on actual patients. No one would be concealing it, least of all the manufacturer. There would be hourly ads on television. Instead, the manufacturer (Merck) is pleading with the public not to take it unless prescribed.

Ultraviolet radiation

Ultraviolet radiation can destroy both Covid-19 viruses and human cells and can cause cancer. It is the reason for using sunblocks and sunglasses. A recent US president suggested ultraviolet might be administered "through the skin or in some other way…the way it kills it in one minute, that's very powerful". Unfortunately, there is actually no way to expose the entire body to this type of ionizing radiation and it would be too toxic, anyway.

Vitamins

Vitamins are required as part of normal metabolism. There is no good reason why they would have antiviral or anti-inflammatory properties, and they don't.

The parallel with tertiary syphilis

Tertiary syphilis can destroy any organ. Before the mid-twentieth century it was one of history's worst scourges. In the author's personal collection is a 1939 medical textbook that lists five syphilis treatments based on arsenic, three based on bismuth, three based on mercury, and two based on iodine, along with cautions such as "do not mistake arsphenamine for neoarsphenamine - such a mistake will usually mean death to the patient." All of these treatments were toxic and ineffective. Less than ten years later, there was a single treatment that was nearly 100% effective - penicillin.

With Covid-19, we are still in 1939.

CHAPTER 16

PUBLIC HEALTH AND HUMAN RIGHTS

It has been said that man is a rational animal. All my life I have been searching for evidence which could support this.

Bertrand Russell

Summary

Covid-19 is largely spread by persons who don't know they have it, in the form of droplets and aerosols that arise from coughing, sneezing and even normal speech. It is only reasonable to keep your distance from people who appear healthy but have unknown immune status. It is also only reasonable to filter the air you inhale if you are around such people. How these elementary truisms devolved into an argument about human rights is hard to explain.

What is public health?

Public health planning imposes tolerable restrictions on everyone for the greater good of all. Examples are protecting drinking water and eradicating infectious diseases. Restrictions can clash with personal liberties so choices must be made. You can't relieve yourself in the reservoir no matter how convenient it may be. And you can't spread disease to others if there is a simple way to avoid it.

The Covid-19 pandemic; however, has seen large numbers of individuals refuse to participate in public health guidelines because they have decided they value their own "freedom" more than they value other people's health. Protecting public health and protecting individual freedoms are both worthy goals. As with all conflicts, it is necessary to decide which takes precedence. Hopefully, for the next year or two, it can be public health.

Social distancing and human rights

It is common sense to stay away from potential aerosol emitters if you are not immune. A radius of about six feet seems to be a reasonable compromise. This is a direct consequence of Newton's Law of Gravitation as it applies to droplets. It has nothing to do with politics or other human concerns.

Breath filtering and human rights

The value of filtering air that is inhaled or exhaled by you is also plain to see. Filter materials are available that are quite successful in removing droplets and even aerosols as they pass through. The best method would be to hold filter material tightly over your nose and mouth whenever you are in the vicinity of other people. This is inconvenient so a portable breath filter, with ear loops to hold it in place, is an alternative. This method has been used by surgeons and other physicians for a century to protect both themselves and others.

Unfortunately, these portable self-retaining breath filters are commonly referred to by the unfortunate term “mask”, conjuring up visions of bank robberies, kidnappings, subterfuge, concealing one’s identity and public shame. A breath filter in "mask" form is not a disguise. No one would hesitate to use a “mask” for a horrible smell. You would probably not be very happy if your surgeon refused to wear one. It is not a scarlet letter or a badge of infamy. In the age of facial recognition software, under different circumstances, it might even be seen as a revolt against state authority. The goal of removing droplets and aerosols with a filtering "mask" was never intended to force people to hide their identity, conceal the essence of their being, sacrifice their individualism or violate their basic human rights. Sometimes a filter is just a filter.

If you find the argument in favour of filtering what you inhale to be reasonable, then the Silver Rule dictates you should provide this protection to others as well by filtering what you exhale.[1]

---

1. The Silver Rule states that is if there is something you don’t want other people to do to you, then don’t do it to them.

CHAPTER 17
OPINIONS

> I THINK THE SUBJECT WHICH WILL BE OF MOST IMPORTANCE POLITICALLY IS MASS PSYCHOLOGY...ITS IMPORTANCE HAS BEEN ENORMOUSLY INCREASED BY THE GROWTH OF MODERN METHODS OF PROPAGANDA. ALTHOUGH THIS SCIENCE WILL BE DILIGENTLY STUDIED, IT WILL BE RIGIDLY CONFINED TO THE GOVERNING CLASS. THE POPULACE WILL NOT BE ALLOWED TO KNOW HOW ITS CONVICTIONS ARE GENERATED.
>
> BERTRAND RUSSELL

One of the biggest problems facing a vaccine-hesitant person is who to believe. Every possible opinion has been expressed by someone, somewhere, including scientists, politicians, Big Pharma, alternative medicine merchants, religious leaders, social influencers, media personalities, striving academics, and even supposed doctors hawking products on television.

A full discussion is beyond the scope of this book. However, there are two questions you might want to use as screening tests.

Credentials and motivations

The first is whether the person expressing an opinion has the necessary education. If not, then the opinion is probably worth what you paid for it. As Napoleon said, "In politics, stupidity is not a handicap".

The second is to ask what hidden motivations the expresser of opinion might have. Honorable motives would include altruism and a search for truth. If these are not plainly in evidence, then the reason may be less praiseworthy and quite possibly concealed. The possibilities would include money, fame, keeping a job, social standing, votes, or a desire to make life more easily comprehensible. In the worst case, demagogues create for themselves a constituency that only they can nurture and lead, knowing full well their exhortations will lead to needless deaths.

Politicians trying to convince you of opposite things is not a new problem. Punch May 31, 1922.

Individuals with narcissistic or sociopathic personality can be as deadly as Covid-19. They really do not care what happens to you as long as it serves their purposes. Such people tend to be quite successful in society. They are often very personable, and masters of faking knowledge and empathy.

Some of the more credentialed and altruistic of public personalities include Dr. Sanjay Gupta, Dr. Peter Hotez, Dr. Isaac Bogoch, Dr. Leana Wen and Dr. Ashish Jha. All are practicing physicians who understand the problem and seem to be motivated by truth rather than personal gain, with an ability to explain things clearly.

"Submit your judgement with modesty"

So said George Washington, who declined to express firm opinions on matters he knew little about.

Unfortunately, a person's level of education, and whether they happen to be right or wrong, is often less important than what they do when they see a microphone. Too many people, in spite of minimal scientific or medical knowledge, will turn towards it rather than away. Many make their living this way.

Not knowing the limits of one's own expertise is always a problem. Knowing the limits, but expressing opinions anyway, is ignorant. Doing this to an audience that is primed to uncritically accept your opinions, and who may die as a result, is abhorrent. This practice has been a major obstacle to achieving herd immunity (discussed in Chapter 20).

Currently, 44% of the US population and 25% of the Canadian population are not fully vaccinated. They make up the bulk of hospital admissions. If they took action tomorrow, in about two weeks both countries would have achieved herd immunity and the Covid-19 crisis would fizzle out.

All deaths are tragic, including the three related below. None of these people had bad intentions, they were just wrong. All had firmly held opinions, based on nothing, about Covid-19 and vaccines. All had many loyal supporters. And all spent their last days in an ICU, connected to a ventilator and other equipment, in pain, sedated and isolated.

. . .

PHIL VALENTINE, 1959-2021

Conservative radio host Phil Valentine died of Covid-19 in August 2021. He compared vaccination status badges to Hitler's yellow stars. Once sick with Covid-19, he self-medicated with vitamin D and ivermectin.[1] He was intubated on July 28, started on ECMO[2] on July 30, and died on August 21. His brother, Mark Valentine said, "I know if he were able to tell you this, he would tell you, 'Go get vaccinated'. Quit worrying about the politics. Quit worrying about all thc conspiracy theories...He regrets not being more adamant about getting the vaccine. Look at the dadgum data."

LANDON SPRADLIN, 1953-2020

Pastor and talented musician Landon Spradlin died of Covid-19 in March 2020. He was a member of the Blues Hall of Fame in Memphis, Tennessee. He preached that the media would "manipulate your life" by creating "mass hysteria" about Covid-19. After performing several outdoor sets in New Orleans during Mardi Gras, he left in his pickup truck for his home in Gretna, Virginia. He was intubated in North Carolina and was soon on kidney dialysis as well. He died 8 days later.

DICK FARREL, 1956-2021

Successful radio host Dick Farrel called Covid-19 a “scamdemic” and masks "face diapers." He described Dr. A. Fauci as a “power-tripping lying freak” who conspired with “power trip lib loons”. In June 2021, he told his listeners not to get vaccinated. Shortly afterwards, he contracted Covid-19. His friends said that, in his last days, he privately urged them to get vaccinated, and some did. Dick Farrel died of Covid in August 2021.

---

1. See Chapter 20.
2. See Chapter 15.

CHAPTER 18

WAS TIME LOST?

IF I WERE TO SUGGEST THAT BETWEEN THE EARTH AND MARS THERE IS A CHINA TEAPOT REVOLVING ABOUT THE SUN IN AN ELLIPTICAL ORBIT, NOBODY WOULD BE ABLE TO DISPROVE MY ASSERTION PROVIDED I WERE CAREFUL TO ADD THAT THE TEAPOT IS TOO SMALL TO BE REVEALED EVEN BY OUR MOST POWERFUL TELESCOPES.

BERTRAND RUSSELL

When did the pandemic actually start?

Government departments tasked with public health, and the World Health Organization (WHO), need to be constantly alert to new diseases like Covid-19. Were they?

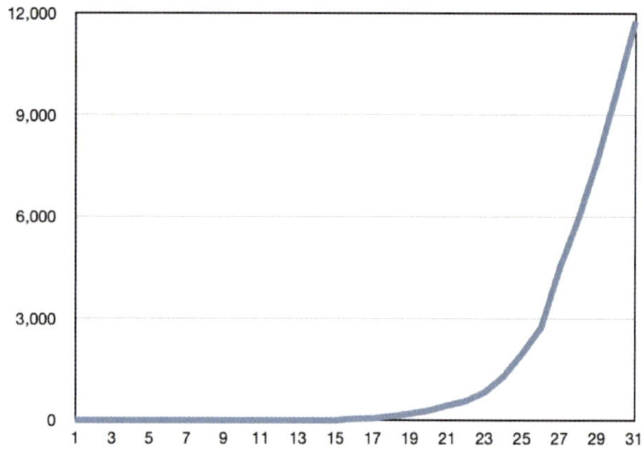

The extremely rapid spread of Covid-19 in China from January 1-31, 2020 (data from WHO, as supplied by China).

Covid-19 is often said to have started in February 2020 but it was actually earlier as the above graph shows. After January 16, 2020, the tally for any particular day is almost exactly 1.5 times that of the previous day, which is the very definition of "exponential".[1]

It should have been clear by the end of January 2020 that, if no effective measures were immediately undertaken, this was going to infect the entire world. What was the world response?

In the United States, there were presidential statements that it was not a problem (January 31), that it was vanishing (February 26) and that it was a hoax (February 28).

Canada was also caught napping. In 2019, the Global Public Health Intelligence Network (GPHIN) was disbanded because there had not been any pandemics lately (!). In the preceding 20 years, independent scientists at GPHIN had helped alert the world to the SARS, MERS, H1N1 influenza, and Ebola epidemics.

Even the WHO could not bring itself to formally acknowledge that we were in a pandemic until March 2020, at which point there were over 100,000 cases in over 100 countries, with continued exponential growth.

By the time infections soared in Canada and the US, authorities were again caught flatfooted by not having enough personal protective equipment (PPE) for hospitals. Top public health officials in both countries claimed, possibly to divert attention from this troubling lack of foresight, that masks were a bad idea anyway as they would just make people touch their faces.

Have governments learned?

It appears that some governments are still feeling their way, caught between the competing poles of public health, individual freedom, business needs and (as always) votes in the next election. In various North American jurisdictions, public health measures are periodically relaxed and then followed by new waves of infection.

In 2020, a radiologist with no qualifications in public health or infectious disease was appointed to the President's Coronavirus Task Force, then concurred with opposing public health measures.[2]

In Brazil, a populist president openly flouted public health measures until getting Covid-19 himself, and even after. Largely as a result of this one person, Brazil has been one of the most severely affected countries.

In August 2021, the Alberta government stated that it planned to cancel nurses' holidays, force them to work overtime, and cut their salaries by over 5% - all at the same time, only to retract it later.

---

1. Exponential growth is when each new population is a constant multiple of the previous one. Compound interest is a familiar example. The constant factor is called R0, which was about 1.5 for Covid-19 in January 2020, but has been as high as 7 at other times and has averaged 2-3 over the 1.5 pandemic years so far.
2. He at least acknowledged the pandemic existed, but thought a good policy would be to let it run its course unrestricted, rather like the bubonic plague in the 1300s.

CHAPTER 19

WHAT COMES NEXT?

MEN FEAR THOUGHT AS THEY FEAR NOTHING ELSE ON EARTH -- MORE THAN RUIN, MORE EVEN THAN DEATH. THOUGHT IS SUBVERSIVE AND REVOLUTIONARY, DESTRUCTIVE AND TERRIBLE, THOUGHT IS MERCILESS TO PRIVILEGE, ESTABLISHED INSTITUTIONS, AND COMFORTABLE HABITS; THOUGHT IS ANARCHIC AND LAWLESS, INDIFFERENT TO AUTHORITY, CARELESS OF THE WELL-TRIED WISDOM OF THE AGES. THOUGHT LOOKS INTO THE PIT OF HELL AND IS NOT AFRAID ... THOUGHT IS GREAT AND SWIFT AND FREE, THE LIGHT OF THE WORLD, AND THE CHIEF GLORY OF MAN.

BERTRAND RUSSELL

Exponential growth is impressive. Many people have heard of the Persian chessboard that starts with a single grain of rice on the first square. Each additional square then receives twice what the previous square had, creating the series 1-2-4-8-16-32, etc. The last square receives approximately 18,446,744,073,709,551,616 ($2^{64)}$ grains of rice. This is exponential growth with an R0 of 2. If the original

Wuhan strain of Covid-19 had continued to grow with its January 2020 reproduction number of 1.5 (see Chapter 18), the entire mass of the Earth would be converted to Covid-19 viruses after only 130 growth cycles.

This is impossible, of course, as resources (i.e., humans) would run out before then. Accurate mathematical modelling of a pandemic is complex and beyond the scope of this book, but here are a few qualitative thought experiments.

Six thought experiments

Thought experiment 1

Assume that every person in the US is susceptible to Covid-19 and is freely breathing the exhaled air of other people, with no breath filtering or distancing. Any given infected person will be surrounded by susceptible people. After 30 days, the originally infected people would be either immune and no longer shedding virus, or dead. But by then many more people would be in the early stages of infection, including asymptomatic spreading to others. This thought experiment results in an unstable and explosive spread of infection, more or less as we have seen at the beginning of every "wave" so far.

Thought experiment 2

Now assume every person in the US agreed to quarantine themselves tomorrow for a month, no matter what their state of health. Those infected would not be surrounded by anyone at all, so the virus could not spread. After 14 days, those originally infected would have either generated their own immune response or died. After 30 days, all the originally infected people that had not died would have conquered the virus, now be immune, and no longer be shedding virus. The contagion would be over.

. . .

Thought experiment 3

This time, let's assume that every person in the US continued to mingle with others for a month, but that 90% of the population was immunized by vaccination. Any given infected person would no longer be surrounded by very many susceptible people, perhaps passing it on to one more person. After 30 days, the originally infected people would either be immune and no longer shedding virus, or dead. On their heels would be one more person in the early stages of infection, asymptomatically spreading and waiting for symptoms to start. This situation would result in a constant, low level of disease that does not spread exponentially. Covid-19 would have become endemic, like malaria in Africa. In this case herd immunity was reached at 90%.

Thought experiment 4

What happens if the vaccination rate is intermediate? Let's assume every person in the US mingles freely with others for a month but that 50% of them are immunized by vaccination. This results in an intermediate situation where, as each of the originally infected people recovers or dies, more than one new case has been created. Mid-level population immunity has slowed the exponential spread of infection but did not stabilize it. Covid-19 will continue to propagate until 90% of the population is either immune or dead.

Thought experiment 5

This time assume the same conditions of thought experiment 4 (i.e. 50% vaccination level) but now with a virus that has mutated to spread twice as fast, as Delta did with respect to the original Wuhan strain. Each infected person, in their asymptomatic phase, will now infect more new people than in thought experiment 4. The rate of spread will be faster, still exponential but also still somewhat constrained by population immunity.

. . .

THOUGHT EXPERIMENT 6

Finally, the nightmare scenario. Assume the virus from thought experiment 5, which has already mutated to spread faster (like Delta), now mutates again so that our IgG antibodies no longer recognize it. No one who survived Covid-19 is immune anymore. No one who was vaccinated is immune, either. The virus is back, more powerful than ever, with a wide open field.

Using the example of Chapter 4, we could imagine the spike protein now looks like a football that the ACE2 receptor catcher's mitt still catches but the IgG pitcher's mitt cannot catch. The new mutation would still spread from a single point source, but faster than the original Wuhan strain. If this happens, it is possible that the only solution will be the medieval one - the disease runs rampant and after a few years the only people left standing are Covid survivors.

What are the chances of scenario 6? Mutation occurs at a constant rate. A small number of Covid-19 viruses will not generate many viable mutants, but a world full of them might. We don't know if there is a possible conformation of the Covid-19 spike protein that will actually be able to fit the ACE2 receptor while evading the IgG antibodies, but if there is, natural selection will probably find it.

Thinking two steps ahead

There is only one practical way to lower this risk and that is by lowering the number of Covid-19 viruses in the world. It does not matter what country the mutation first occurs in, if it occurs anywhere it will spread like wildfire. We have already seen the original strain spread from China, the Alpha variant spread from Britain, the Beta variant spread from South Africa, the Gamma variant spread from Brazil, and the disastrous Delta variant spread from India. Delta is the most infectious and rapidly growing variant and has now taken over most of the world. Covid-19 does not recognize borders.

Thinking two steps ahead might prevent this, but thinking only one step ahead will likely fail. As long as we obsess about third or fourth booster doses for developed countries, we will not achieve the necessary reduction in world virus numbers that first doses to poorer countries would accomplish. It is in everyone's best interests, everywhere in the world, to get first doses into everyone as the true priority.

Coffin transportation, 1918 influenza pandemic.

CHAPTER 20

OTHER ISSUES

> WHY REPEAT THE OLD ERRORS, IF THERE ARE SO MANY NEW ERRORS TO COMMIT?
>
> BERTRAND RUSSELL

In this chapter, breathing filters will be called masks and spike protein training will be called vaccination.

Is Covid-19 continuing to evolve?

The Center for Disease Control's four "variants of concern" are Alpha (previously called the UK variant or B.1.1.7); Beta (previously called South Africa variant or B.1.351); Gamma (previously called the Brazil variant or P.1), and Delta (previously called the Indian variant or B.1.617.2). The current names reflect the fact that all of them affect the entire world.

In addition to these four "variants of concern", CDC is monitoring 16 "variants of interest", all of which have spike protein mutations. So far they are all susceptible to current vaccines. There will be more.

Will there be entirely new coronaviruses in the future?

Three virulent coronaviruses have emerged in the last 20 years. Severe Acute Respiratory Syndrome (SARS) killed 774 people, MERS (Middle East Respiratory Syndrome) killed 866 people, and Covid-19 has killed 4,500,000 and counting. They appear to have crossed into humans from various mammals including civet cats, camels, pangolins and bats. If this is a pattern, there will presumably be more.

Is there a single statistic to remember?

At the time of writing, one statistic says it all - the great majority of Covid-19 patients on ventilators are unvaccinated.

How can we use vaccines without a track history of safety?

We make decisions every day based on incomplete evidence. It has also never been scientifically proven that operating on appendicitis saves lives, but there are good reasons to think it does. If we were to insist on definitive evidence that there will be no vaccine safety concerns 10 years from now, we may die waiting. The evidence, while not conclusive, is persuasive so far that the vaccines are safe.[1]

How is Covid-19 different from seasonal influenza, SARS and Ebola?

Covid-19

- 100 patients will infect up to 700 more;
- 2 of the 100 will die, including people who were previously healthy;

- Victims will often not be aware they are infected and remain active, spreading the contagion;
- Spread is explosive and can overwhelm hospitals;
- Severe Covid-19 patients are often otherwise healthy and therefore good candidates for ventilators, if any are available.

Seasonal influenza

- 100 patients will infect up to 150 more;
- Outbreaks vary by the year and are not usually pandemics, but typically about 1 in 1,000 infected patients die, mostly people who are old and/or chronically ill. In the most severe forms, up to 75 of every 100 infected people die[2];
- Victims are usually aware they are infected and are less likely to be active, so spread is less explosive than Covid-19;
- Because many victims are elderly or chronically ill, artificial ventilation may not be in their best interests so there is less demand for ventilators.

SARS (2002)

- 100 patients will infect up to 300 more;
- 10 of the 100 will die;
- Victims are very sick and hospitalized early, so asymptomatic spreading is less than Covid-19.

Ebola

- 100 patients will infect up to 200 more;
- 40 of the 100 will die;
- Victims are extremely sick and hospitalized early, so asymptomatic spreading is less than Covid-19.

Has the healthcare system been overwhelmed?

In poorer countries without much oxygen or many hospital beds, this has obviously been the case. In the US and other developed countries, it depends on what you consider adequate health care to be. In normal times if you have pneumonia with impending respiratory failure, you will be on a ventilator for a week or two until your lungs recover. Currently, with Covid-19, you might have to gasp for every breath, as if you were being suffocated, for days or weeks before another patient dies and their ventilator becomes available to you. If you ultimately survive this, will you say the system functioned as it should or that it failed you?

What is herd immunity?

Herd immunity occurs when each infected person passes a disease on to zero or one new person, so that exponential growth does not occur. It is probably achieved at around 80-90% immunity. The immunity can be from mass vaccination or by letting the disease run rampant until the only people left standing are those that had it, survived, and are now immune. One is civilized and the other a throwback to medieval times.

The extremely contagious disease measles has been curtailed for decades by herd immunity, with nearly 100% vaccination. However, in 2018 in Samoa, the vaccination level fell to around 30% and over 5,700 measles cases quickly occurred. The epidemic stopped when the vaccination rate went up again.[3] Nearby islands, like Nauru and the Cook Islands, maintained herd immunity levels and had no outbreak.

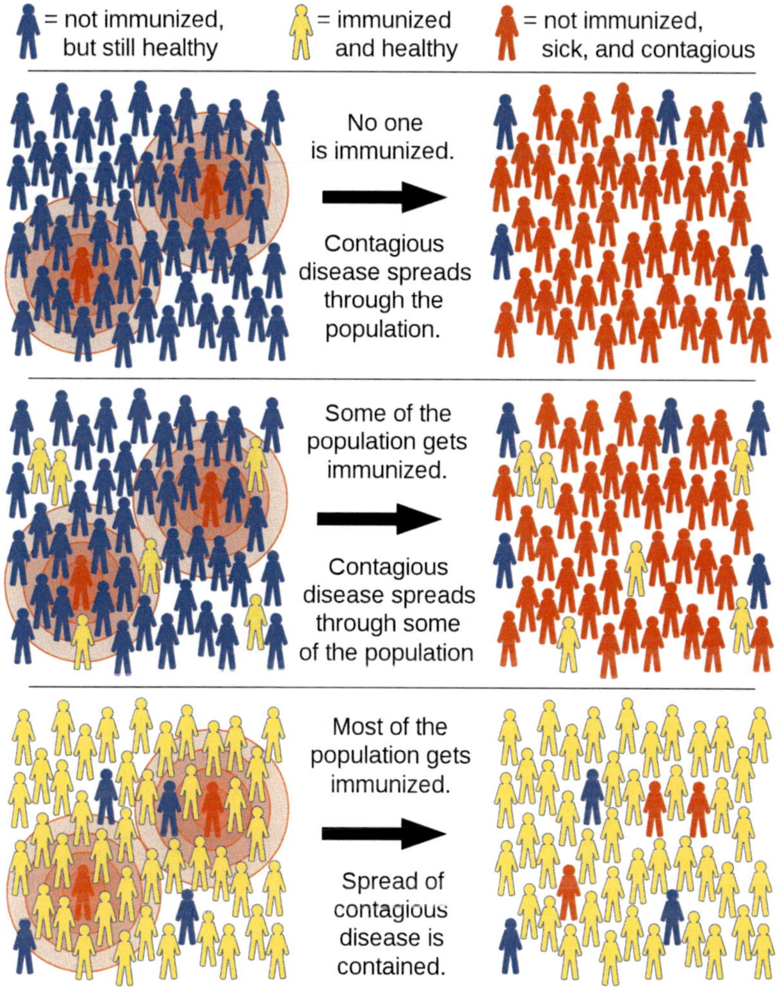

Herd immunity means almost everyone is immune.

What is it like to have severe Covid-19?

One recent survivor was quoted on TV as saying it was like having a Ziploc bag over her head for two weeks. Others have likened it to drowning. A recent vice-president might compare it to waterboarding. Being unable to breathe is an agonizing and terrifying experience.

Is Covid-19 a medical hoax?

It is impossible to imagine that scientists, physicians and the media are conspiring to make it appear there is a pandemic that is actually not there. Pandemics are not something new, just new in the personal experience of most people alive today. Covid-19 is not a hoax.

Do Covid-19 vaccines contain microchips?

In May 2020, Roman Catholic Cardinal R. Burke, a man known more for his grasp of theology than his scientific training, opposed vaccination and said (amongst other things) that vaccines might contain microchips "so that at any moment he or she can be controlled regarding health and regarding other matters, which we can only imagine as a possible object of control by the state." He is currently recovering in hospital from his week on a ventilator.

The idea seems implausible. What would be the energy source allowing these chips to broadcast to the nearest government receiver? How would the chips control human physiology, behaviour or thinking? How would such an intense collaboration between computer companies and vaccine developers be kept secret? How could microchips be injected when they are larger than the needles? Why are there no unaltered photos of actual microchips in vaccines?

Will doctors and nurses burn out?

Hospital medicine and nursing in critical care areas are labor-intensive and emotionally taxing. Many doctors and nurses are already stressed to the point of wanting to quit. Virtually all of them believe that Covid-19 is not a hoax and that vaccinations are the way forward. This makes it difficult, at times, for them to empathize with critically ill patients who insist they know better.

Do masks cause carbon dioxide poisoning?

A face mask cannot give you carbon dioxide poisoning as it does not retain your exhaled air in a bag. Surgeons and other doctors have been using masks since the days of Joseph Lister and Louis Pasteur, over 100 years ago, without poisoning themselves.

What is a reasonable breath filter?

A certified N95 mask with a middle polypropylene layer and a metal strip to shape it over the nose is thought to be quite effective in removing droplet and aerosol particles but is not perfect. There should be no exhalation valve if you want to protect others. Makeshift bandanas or scarves have large pore sizes that do not stop aerosols. Face shields redirect air flow and may protect you from big splashes but do not filter.

Industrial or medical N95 masks are said to work well. A vacuum cleaner HEPA filtration bag is probably better than nothing (make sure it does not contain any fiberglass first). Even a tissue is more effective than nothing.

Filtration material can be simply held against the face. Manufactured inhalation filters with ear loops (somewhat misleadingly called "masks") are convenient but often fit loosely and allow air to enter through the sides. This is a serious flaw but they are still better than nothing. You should either purchase ones that are molded more anatomically to the face or hold the filter against your face by hand at times of possible high exposure. To test the seal, inhale sharply (sniff) to see if the mask is sucked towards your face.

There are very few legitimate medical contraindications to wearing a mask.

If you use an inhalation/exhalation filter of any type, mask or otherwise, it is still wise to also use other reasonable precautions like staying upwind of other people, maintaining good building ventilation, and keeping your distance from possible sources.

Should children wear masks?

Children infected with Covid-19 are often asymptomatic but they generate lots of aerosols while talking, laughing or screaming with delight on the playground. A few will become sick or even die. Many, perhaps most, will also shed Covid-19 virus around susceptible adults, including their parents.

Some politicians rail against the sight of children being required to wear masks and hide their smiles. No one wants to see masked children, but it is better than seeing orphans. It's not forever.

Fear of needles

Fear of needles is common. Most of the pain comes from piercing the skin. The skin can be numbed with EMLA cream for one hour before the injection. EMLA is a commonly used local anesthetic formulated for topical (skin) use.

Is a virus alive?

Life is said to require three things - the ability to reproduce, some type of barrier to protect the organism from the elements and parasites, and a means of extracting energy from the environment. Covid-19 cannot accomplish these without taking over a cell. It steals energy and chemical compounds from the cell it invades, and is therefore not alive in the usual sense.

Recently, viruses that live inside of other viruses have even been discovered, an interesting situation of one non-living entity parasitizing another non-living entity.

Do vaccines harm pregnancies?

Covid-19 vaccines do not accumulate in the ovaries and the ovaries do not start producing spike protein themselves, as some have claimed. At the state of current medical knowledge, the vaccines do not cause miscarriages above the usual rate of about 12.5%, do not cause fetal malformations, and do not raise antibodies against the fetus or placenta. Covid-19 (the disease) appears to be much more likely than any of the vaccines to kill mothers during pregnancy .

Do long-term carriers exist for Covid-19?

So far there is no evidence that a person can be in a state of permanent asymptomatic spreading, as with "Typhoid Mary."[4]

What factors increase the risk of dying from Covid-19?

The following factors make your prognosis worse (these are not necessarily independent): age, male sex, diabetes, underlying respiratory disease, smoking, underlying heart disease, being immunosuppressed, high blood pressure and having underlying cancer.

What was the Great Barrington Declaration of 2020?

This brief manifesto was signed by a zoologist, a non-practicing physician and a math professor in Great Barrington, Massachusetts, the birthplace of Laura Secord. It recommended that people take no Covid-

19 precautions so that the Covid-19 virus could spread freely and eventually result in herd immunity, somewhat like the Black Death of the Middle Ages.

Lawyer Alex Azar, the Chairman of the White House Coronavirus Task Force at the time, said it "matches the policy of the president". Dr. A. Fauci called it "nonsense and very dangerous". The WHO Director called it "scientifically and ethically problematic."

Is Covid-19 a bioweapon?

Many people have speculated that Covid-19 was accidentally released from the Wuhan Institute of Virology, which was close to the outbreak centre. China, in response, has suggested the US developed Covid-19 and deliberately spread it from that part of Wuhan to make it look like China's fault.

Neither country has denied having biological weapons. China has not denied the Wuhan Institute of Virology is involved in bioweapons. Neither has denied working on coronaviruses as bioweapons.

On the other hand, there are plenty of other viruses and bacteria that are more lethal. Covid-19 is difficult to "weaponize" as it does not tolerate dryness very well, compared to anthrax spores or plague-infected fleas. Deliberately using a highly contagious bioweapon during peacetime on a 21st century internationally-mobile population would carry an unthinkably high risk of spreading back to the aggressor.[5]

The main alternate explanation relates to a "wet market" situated in the same Wuhan neighborhood, where domestic and wild animals are vivisected, killed and dismembered under conditions many would consider both unsanitary and inhumane. Under these conditions, countless droplets and aerosols are in direct contact with humans. They provide exotic meat to those who want it, and the pangolin scales are said to promote "circulation." Thankfully, in 2020 China removed pangolin scales from the official state pharmacopoeia.

Is natural immunity better than artificial?

Immunity simply means our immune system has learned to recognize the Covid-19 virus's spike protein and immediately fight it to the floor. It takes about 14 days for this learning to occur from the time of first exposure. The nature of your virgin experience with spike protein might determine your fate. If it comes from the Covid-19 virus itself, you might get very sick, infect your family and even die. If it comes from a bottle, you might have a sore arm for a day. The antibodies are the same either way.

Did God create Covid-19 for a reason?

This question is beyond the scope of this book, as is the related question, "Did God create scientists for a reason?"

Who was Bertrand Russell?

Bertrand Russell was an aristocratically born Englishman who lived from 1872 to 1970. His academic work concerned mathematics and philosophy. He also spoke out freely and eloquently about foolish ideas, political correctness, hypocrisy, cruelty and stupidity in all its many forms.

In 1916, he was fired by Cambridge University for opposing World War I. In 1950 he was awarded the Nobel Prize in Literature. In 1955, he and Albert Einstein produced the Russell-Einstein Manifesto calling for a complete ban on nuclear weapons. At age 89, in 1961, he was imprisoned for one week for protesting nuclear weapons after he refused an offer to avoid jail by promising future good behavior. Bertrand Russell died during a pandemic.

Bertrand Russell

LOVE IS WISE; HATRED IS FOOLISH. IN THIS WORLD, WHICH IS GETTING MORE AND MORE CLOSELY INTERCONNECTED, WE HAVE TO LEARN TO TOLERATE EACH OTHER, WE HAVE TO LEARN TO PUT UP WITH THE FACT THAT SOME PEOPLE SAY THINGS THAT WE DON'T LIKE. WE CAN ONLY LIVE TOGETHER IN THAT WAY. BUT IF WE ARE TO LIVE TOGETHER, AND NOT DIE TOGETHER, WE MUST LEARN A KIND OF CHARITY AND A KIND OF TOLERANCE, WHICH IS ABSOLUTELY VITAL TO THE CONTINUATION OF HUMAN LIFE ON THIS PLANET.

1. The example that has wired generations was the Salk polio vaccine from the 1950s, made from killed polio viruses. It turned out to also contain another virus, SV-40, that was not killed. Many children, the author included, received this vaccine. So far it has not caused a problem. Modern mRNA vaccines and adenovirus vaccines are known to be much purer and are extremely unlikely to contain any other viruses.
2. The 1918 "Spanish flu" (H1N1) pandemic killed about 10 of every 100 infected patients. The 1957-58 "Asian flu" (H2N2) was also a pandemic but killed only 1 in 1,000 patients. The 1968-69 "Hong Kong flu" pandemic (H3N2) killed 1 of every 500 infected people, which was still one million deaths worldwide. "Bird flu" (H5N1) has not yet caused a pandemic, but it will be fearsome if and when it does - whenever it crops up it kills up to 75 of every 100 infected people.
3. The situation started when two children died because their vaccine was negligently mixed with another drug that paralyzed breathing, instead of with water. The children died after a vaccination, but not because of the vaccine itself. A local coconut farmer with internet skills then convinced a large segment of the population that vaccination was the cause of death and should be avoided.
4. Mary Mallon had typhoid bacteria living in her at all times but was healthy. Unfortunately, 53 people who crossed paths with her either as a restaurant cook or as a governess died. After a lengthy chase and quarantine period, and based on her promise never to cook for the public again if released, she was freed and promptly got a job at a restaurant. More people died. She was tracked down once again and this time isolated on a New York prison island for the last 30 years of her life. She died in 1938, four years before the first successful clinical use of an antibiotic.

   Covid-19 carriers are people who shed Covid-19 virus without being sick themselves. This is common in the early stages of infection but, so far at least, seems to be self-limited. Eventually, the immune system seems to exterminate the Covid-19. It does not persist and shed for decades, as Typhoid Mary's typhoid bacterium did.
5. Bioweapons exist in many countries but are difficult to use due to the risk of infecting the aggressor's own population. During World War II, Japan intended to release bubonic plague in California as "Operation Cherry Blossoms at Night" - whether it would have eventually reached back to the Japanese home islands is unknown. The atomic bombs in August 1945 prevented this plan from being carried out.

   In preparation, up to half a million Chinese civilians were directly infected with bubonic plague, cholera, botulism, smallpox, anthrax, dysentery and/or typhoid for practice. The diseases were not widely dispersed but rather captives, referred to as rogu ("logs"), were infected under conditions that allowed the vivisectionists to avoid getting infected themselves. A later trial of mass delivery backfired when close to 20% of the Japanese soldiers became infected.

   Mass dispersal biological attacks also occurred in 1710 when Russians catapulted the bodies of plague victims into Tallinn, Estonia, and by the British who gave smallpox-infected blankets to North American First Nations.

IMAGE CREDITS

CHAPTER 2:

- James Gathany (https://commons.wikimedia.org/wiki/File:Sneeze.JPG) „Sneeze" marked as public domain more details on Wikimedia Commons: https://commons.wikimedia.org/wiki/Template:PD-US
- Patrick J. Lynch medical illustrator (https://commons.wikimedia.org/wiki/File:Head_lateral_mouth_anatomy.jpg) "Head lateral mouth anatomy" https://creativecommons.org/licenses/by/2.5/legalcode
- Dr. Yeolkyo Choi.
- Christinelmiller (https://commons.wikimedia.org/wiki/File:Protein_Synthesis_Elongation.png) https://creativecommons.org/licenses/by-sa/4.0/legalcode
- Creative Commons Attribution License (CC-BY 4.0; https://creativecommons.org/licenses/by/4.0/legalcode).
- Alexey Solodovnikov (Idea, Producer, CG, Editor), Valeria Arkhipova (Scientific Consultant) (https://commons.wikimedia.org/wiki/File:Coronavirus._SARS-CoV-2.png), https: // creativecommons. org / licenses / by-sa / 4.0 / legalcode
- National Institute of Allergy and Infectious Diseases

CHAPTER 3

Wykis (https://commons.wikimedia.org/wiki/File:Antibiotic_resistance.svg), “Antibiotic resistance”, marked as public domain, details on Wikimedia Commons: https://commons.wikimedia.org/wiki/Template:PD -self

Chapter 4

- Lisa Donohue, CoVPN

Chapter 5

- Photo: <a href="https://foto.wuestenigel.com/the-concept-of-a-healthy-planet-no-pollution-and-disease/" target="_blank">The concept of a healthy planet

Chapter 6

- Adenovirus_Kapsid_01.jpg: Self-drawn Gleiberg derivative work: Hic et nunc (https://commons.wikimedia.org/wiki/File:Adenovirus_Kapsid_01.png) “Adenovirus Kapsid 01” https://creativecommons.org/licenses/by -sa / 2.0 / de / legalcode
- Christinelmiller (https://commons.wikimedia.org/wiki/File:Messenger_RNA_-_Simple.png), https://creativecommons.org/licenses/by-sa/4.0/legalcode
- Katie L. Flanagan, Emma Best, Nigel W. Crawford, Michelle Giles, Archana Koirala, Kristine Macartney, Fiona Russell, Benjamin W. Teh, and Sophie CH Wen, on behalf of the Australasian Society for Infectious Diseases (ASID) Vaccination Special Interest group (VACSIG) (https://commons.wikimedia.org/wiki/File:Fimmu-11-579250-g004.jpg), https://creativecommons.org/licenses/by/4.0/legalcode

Chapter 12

- Personeoneste (https://commons.wikimedia.org/wiki/File:Dice.svg), „Dice“, marked as public domain, more details on Wikimedia Commons: https://commons.wikimedia.org/wiki/Template:PD-self
- Peter Rimar (https://commons.wikimedia.org/wiki/File:ICU1a.jpg), „ICU1a“, marked as public domain, more details on Wikimedia Commons: https://commons.wikimedia.org/wiki/Template:PD-user

Chapter 13

- Mikael Häggström, M.D. - Author info - Reusing images Mikael Häggström (https://commons.wikimedia.org/wiki/File:Symptoms_of_coronavirus_disease_2019_4.0.svg), „Symptoms of coronavirus disease 2019 4.0", https://creativecommons.org/publicdomain/zero/1.0/legalcode
- Central Hematology Laboratory Hemostasis Research Laboratory Bern University Hospital & University of Bern (https://commons.wikimedia.org/wiki/File:Blood_smear_with_typical_schistocytes_in_TTP_marked_in_blue_1.tif), https://creativecommons.org/licenses/by-sa/4.0/legalcode

Chapter 17

- Tkarcher (https://commons.wikimedia.org/wiki/File:Herd_immunity.svg), https://creativecommons.org/licenses/by-sa/4.0/legalcode

Made in the USA
Middletown, DE
01 October 2021

49441606R00075